Summary

Chapter 1: The Origins of Herbal Medicine

The practice of herbal medicine is deeply rooted in human history, dating back thousands of years to ancient civilizations such as the Egyptians, Greeks, and Chinese. These cultures recognized the healing power of plants and utilized various botanical remedies to treat ailments and promote well-being. In this chapter, we will embark on a journey through time and explore the fascinating origins of herbal medicine, delving into the wisdom, knowledge, and practices passed down through the ages.

Ancient Egypt: The Birthplace of Herbal Healing

Our exploration of herbal medicine begins in the land of the pharaohs, ancient Egypt. Egyptians regarded plants as sacred gifts from the gods, with medicinal properties that could cure diseases and promote longevity. Papyrus scrolls, such as the Ebers Papyrus, dating back to 1550 BCE, contain extensive information about herbal remedies and their application. Egyptians used various herbs like aloe vera, myrrh, and frankincense to treat ailments ranging from skin disorders to digestive issues. The physicians of ancient Egypt were revered for their knowledge of these botanical remedies and played a crucial role in the vital healthcare system of their time.

Ancient Greece: The Birth of Herbal Science

As we journey forward in time, we arrive in ancient Greece, the birthplace of modern medicine. Greek philosopher-physicians like Hippocrates and Dioscorides revolutionized the study of herbs, categorizing them based on their properties and uses. Hippocrates, often referred to as the "Father of Medicine," emphasized the concept of the body's natural healing ability and believed that herbal remedies were instrumental in supporting this inherent capacity. His teachings led to the establishment of a system called humoral medicine, which centered around balancing the body's four humors – blood, phlegm, yellow bile, and black bile. This system guided the use of herbs to restore balance and promote health.

Dioscorides, a notable Greek physician and pharmacologist, penned De Materia Medica, an influential medical text that remained the standard reference for herbal medicine well into the Middle Ages. This encyclopedic work documented over 600 medicinal plants and their properties, providing a comprehensive knowledge base for generations of healers to come. From the Greeks, we inherited a legacy of systematic herbal study and an organized approach to botanical medicine that laid the foundation for future advancements.

Ancient China: The Art of Balancing Yin and Yang

Our exploration of herbal medicine now takes us to ancient China, where a philosophical system of health was born. Chinese medicine, deeply rooted in Taoist principles, emphasizes the balance between opposing forces, known as yin and yang. This balance is believed to be essential for maintaining optimal health and preventing disease.

Herbal medicine played a vital role in achieving this equilibrium, with the use of medicinal herbs aimed at harmonizing the body, mind, and spirit.

The oldest surviving text on Chinese herbal medicine, the Huangdi Neijing (Yellow Emperor's Inner Canon), compiled around 200 BCE, outlines the complex theories and treatment protocols of this ancient healing tradition. Herbology in traditional Chinese medicine involved careful observation, diagnosis, and a deep understanding of the energetic properties of plants. Practitioners classified herbs according to their tastes, temperatures, and meridians, identifying their specific effects on the body. Ingredients such as ginseng, ginger, and licorice were frequently used not only to treat illness but also to enhance vitality and prevent disease.

India: Ayurveda, the Science of Life
As we continue our journey, we arrive in ancient India, where Ayurveda, the "Science of Life," flourished. Ayurveda, a holistic system of medicine, encompasses a wide range of approaches, including herbal medicine, diet, yoga, and meditation. Written in the Sanskrit language, the ancient Ayurvedic texts, such as the Charaka Samhita and the Sushruta Samhita, provide comprehensive guidelines for preventive and therapeutic herbal treatments.

Ayurveda considers each individual unique, emphasizing the importance of tailoring treatment plans to restore balance and correct imbalances in the body. Herbs like turmeric, holy basil, and brahmi form the foundation of Ayurvedic herbal medicine, helping to address a vast array of conditions while also promoting overall wellness. Ayurveda's emphasis on the interconnectedness of the mind, body, and spirit paved the way for personalized, holistic healing practices still widely followed today.

In this enlightening journey through time, we have glimpsed into the rich origins of herbal medicine, witnessing its evolution across various ancient civilizations. From the Egyptians' sacred relation to plants to the Greeks' systematic study of herbs, and the Chinese and Indian traditions' emphasis on balance and individuality, herbal medicine has always sought to harness the healing power of nature.

As we delve deeper into subsequent chapters, we will explore the growth and transformation of herbal medicine throughout history, examining its role in medieval Europe, the renaissance of herbalism, and its relevance to modern healthcare practices. The wisdom and knowledge imparted by our ancestors continue to guide us on this path, reminding us of the tremendous potential nature holds in healing and promoting wellness.

Early Human Encounters with Plants

From the very beginning, plants have played a vital role in the lives of humanity. They served as sources of sustenance, medicine, shelter, and even artistic inspiration. In this chapter, we delve into the fascinating story of early human encounters with plants - our ancestors' quest to unlock the secrets held within the green world.

Rise of Homo sapiens:

Around 200,000 years ago, our species, Homo sapiens, emerged in Africa from earlier hominid ancestors. As our early ancestors traversed diverse landscapes, they were exposed to a plethora of plant life, each offering unique potentials and challenges. These first encounters with plants would lay the foundation for our species' relationship with the botanical world.

Discovering Edible Plants:

Food has always been a primary driving force behind human exploration and settlement patterns. Our early ancestors, relying on trial and error, gradually discovered edible plant species that provided them with vital nutrients. Fruits, tubers, nuts, and seeds were particularly crucial in their quest for sustenance.

The Rise of Agriculture:

Around 10,000 years ago, a significant shift in human interaction with plants occurred - the advent of agriculture. Early humans discovered that they could intentionally cultivate certain plant species and create reliable food sources. This agricultural revolution transformed human societies and allowed for the establishment of permanent settlements.

Medicinal Plants and Shamanistic Practices:

Plants not only served as a source of food but also played a pivotal role in ancient medicine. Indigenous cultures worldwide developed a profound understanding of plants' healing properties, leading to the emergence of shamanistic practices. Shaman, the spiritual leaders of their communities, would use various plants to treat ailments and communicate with the spiritual realm.

Psychoactive and Hallucinogenic Plants:

Ancient humans also stumbled upon plants with psychoactive and hallucinogenic properties. Through experimentation, they unearthed their potential, using them for ceremonial purposes, spiritual enlightenment, ánd even artistic inspiration. Many indigenous cultures continue to employ these plants in sacred rituals to this day, preserving ancient knowledge and traditions.

Plant-Based Ceremonies and Rituals:

Plants permeated every aspect of early human society, extending beyond sustenance and medicine. Various ceremonial and religious practices revolved around plants, celebrating their significance in life's cyclic nature. These rituals fostered a profound connection between humans and the botanical world, transcending ordinary existence.

Explorers and the Spice Trade:

Humanity's curiosity and adventurous spirit propelled some individuals to embark on epic journeys in search of new plants and their associated riches. From the ancient Silk Road to the European Age of Exploration, explorers sought valuable spices, medicinal plants, and ornamental flora, sparking cultural exchange and shaping the course of history.

Plant Domestication and Horticulture:

Through careful observation of plant life, early humans recognized the potential for domestication. This pivotal development marked a crucial turning point in our relationship with plants. Humans began to selectively breed and cultivate plants to enhance desirable traits, yielding crops that were more resilient, productive, and nutritionally rich.

Cultural Significance of Plants:

As civilizations flourished, plants became deeply embedded in cultural practices, art, and symbolism. Plants feature prominently in mythologies, sculptures, paintings, and literature, embodying both practical and metaphorical meanings in diverse cultural contexts. Their significance extends beyond physical sustenance, representing life, growth, beauty, and spiritual interconnectedness.

Traditional Herbal Practices Across Cultures

Throughout history, cultures around the world have relied on traditional herbal practices to treat ailments and promote overall well-being. These practices, deeply rooted in ancient traditions and folklore, have been passed down through generations, evolving over time and adapting to different cultural beliefs and environments. In this chapter, we will explore the rich tapestry of traditional herbal practices across various cultures, uncovering the common threads that unite them, as well as the unique aspects that make them distinct.

Ancient Egyptian Medicine:

One of the earliest records of herbal medicine can be traced back to ancient Egypt, where healers used herbs and natural remedies to cure diseases. The Ebers Papyrus, a revered medical document dating back to 1550 BCE, contains extensive information on over 850 plant-based medicines. Egyptians believed that illness resulted from a disruption of the body's balance, and these plant remedies were used to restore equilibrium.

One key herb used in Egyptian medicine was the opium poppy, valued for its analgesic properties. The ancient Egyptians cultivated this plant to relieve pain and induce a state of sedation during surgical procedures. They also used garlic as an antibiotic and antifungal agent, demonstrating a keen understanding of the plant's medicinal properties.

Ancient Chinese Medicine:

China has a long and storied history of herbal medicine that dates back over 5,000 years. Traditional Chinese Medicine (TCM) is based on the concept of Qi, the vital energy that flows through the body, and its balance is essential for health. Chinese medicine utilizes a vast array of herbs, minerals, and animal products to restore balance and promote healing.

The Chinese pharmacopoeia, known as "Shennong Ben Cao Jing," is one of the oldest herbal texts and catalogues over 360 herbs. Among the most famous Chinese herbs is ginseng, renowned for its energy-boosting and immune-enhancing properties. Ginseng is believed to strengthen Qi and is often used as an adaptogen, helping the body cope with stress.

Another essential herb in TCM is astragalus, which is regarded as a powerful immune system booster. For centuries, it has been used in Chinese herbal formulations to help prevent and treat various illnesses.

Indigenous Healing Practices:

Indigenous cultures around the world have long relied on traditional herbal practices for healing and spiritual well-being. These practices are deeply intertwined with their cultural beliefs and traditions, often involving rituals and ceremonies.

In Native American cultures, herbal medicine is known as "plant spirit medicine," where each plant is believed to possess its own unique spirit and healing qualities. The Native Americans use herbs such as sage, sweetgrass, and cedar in smudging ceremonies to cleanse and purify both physical and spiritual energy.

South American indigenous cultures, such as the Amazonian tribes, have a rich tradition of using plants as medicinal remedies. The use of Ayahuasca, a powerful hallucinogenic brew made from a combination of plants, plays a central role in their healing practices. Ayahuasca is believed to connect individuals to the spiritual world, allowing them to gain insight, heal emotional wounds, and treat various ailments.

Traditional African Medicine:

Africa is a vast continent with diverse cultures, each with its unique herbal healing practices. African traditional medicine has its roots in the spiritual belief that illnesses are caused by malevolent spirits or ancestral curses. The healers, often known as traditional doctors or herbalists, combine their knowledge of herbs with spiritual rituals to cure their patients.

One prominent African healing herb is the African Potato (Hypoxis hemerocallidea), widely used to boost the immune system and alleviate symptoms of HIV/AIDS. The herb's tuberous roots are prepared as a medicinal tea or ground into a powder and ingested.

Another notable African medicinal plant is the Rooibos tree, indigenous to the South African Cape region. Rooibos tea, derived from the plant's leaves, is renowned for its antioxidant properties and is used to treat a wide range of ailments, including allergies, digestive disorders, and skin conditions.

Traditional Herbal Practices in India:

India's ancient healing system, Ayurveda, has a profound influence on traditional herbal practices not only within the country but also globally. Ayurveda, which means "The Science of Life," encompasses a holistic approach to health and emphasizes the balance between body, mind, and spirit.

One of the most well-known herbs used in Ayurveda is Turmeric (Curcuma longa), known for its potent anti-inflammatory and antioxidant properties. Turmeric is widely used in Ayurvedic remedies to treat arthritis, digestive disorders, and skin conditions.

Another popular Ayurvedic herb is Ashwagandha (Withania somnifera), considered an adaptogen and used to combat stress and boost energy. It is also believed to improve cognitive function and promote overall vitality.

Traditional herbal practices have stood the test of time, connecting cultures and revealing the deep wisdom our ancestors possessed in treating illnesses and promoting well-being. Despite significant differences, these practices share a common thread, emphasizing the power of nature's pharmacy.

From the ancient Egyptians to Chinese healers, indigenous cultures worldwide, and the Ayurvedic traditions of India, each culture has embraced the healing power of herbs in its unique way. By understanding and respecting the rich tapestry of traditional herbal practices, we can further explore their potential and integrate valuable knowledge into modern medicine, ensuring a cohesive approach that harmonizes both ancient wisdom and scientific advancement.

Evolution of Herbal Knowledge

Throughout history, humans have relied on the healing properties of plants and herbs to treat various ailments and diseases. The development and evolution of herbal knowledge can be traced back to ancient civilizations, where herbal medicine played a central role in their medical practices. This chapter aims to explore the fascinating journey of herbal knowledge, from its early beginnings to the modern era, highlighting the significant discoveries, cultural influences, and the impact it has had on healthcare systems worldwide.

Ancient Civilizations: The Roots of Herbal Medicine

The roots of herbal medicine can be found in the ancient civilizations of Egypt, China, Greece, and India. These cultures extensively documented their knowledge of medicinal plants, serving as a foundation for future generations. In ancient Egypt, papyrus manuscripts like the Ebers Papyrus and the Edwin Smith Papyrus provided valuable insights into the use of herbs for medicinal purposes. The Egyptians believed that plants possessed divine properties and utilized them to cure illnesses and promote overall well-being.

China, known for its rich herbal traditions, gave birth to one of the oldest known books on herbal medicine, the "Shennong Ben Cao

Jing." Compiled during the Han dynasty, this monumental work cataloged around 365 medicinal plants, their properties, and uses. The concept of Yin and Yang and the flow of vital energy, or Qi, heavily influenced Chinese herbal medicine, which continues to thrive to this day.

Greek civilization, led by notable figures such as Hippocrates, made significant contributions to the field of herbal medicine. Hippocrates, often referred to as the "Father of Medicine," emphasized the importance of using plants as medicines and coined the famous phrase, "Let food be thy medicine, and medicine be thy food." Greek herbal knowledge spread throughout the Mediterranean and laid the foundation for many herbal traditions in Europe.

In India, Ayurveda, one of the oldest traditional systems of medicine, prescribed herb-based treatments for a wide range of ailments. The ancient Ayurvedic text "Charaka Samhita" extensively documented the healing properties of various herbs, minerals, and animal products. Ayurvedic principles and practices continue to be widely practiced in India and have gained recognition worldwide.

The Middle Ages: Herbal Wisdom in Monasteries
As the Roman Empire fell and Europe entered the Middle Ages, herbal medicine found refuge within monasteries. Monks played a crucial role in preserving and expanding herbal knowledge during this period. The Benedictine order, in particular, excelled in producing herbal manuscripts, such as the "Hortulus" by Walahfrid Strabo, which provided practical instructions for cultivating and

utilizing medicinal plants.

Monastic gardens became important centers for nurturing and studying plants, with monks carefully categorizing herbs based on their medicinal properties. Herbalists like Hildegard von Bingen, a renowned herbalist, further advanced herbal knowledge with her work, "Physica," which described the therapeutic attributes of over 200 plants.

The Age of Exploration: A Global Exchange of Herbal Knowledge

The Age of Exploration marked a significant turning point in the evolution of herbal knowledge. European explorers ventured to new lands, encountering exotic plants and engaging with indigenous communities, leading to the exchange of herbal knowledge on a global scale. Christopher Columbus' expedition to the Americas, for instance, unveiled an abundance of novel medicinal plants, such as tobacco, cacao, and cinchona bark, which would greatly impact Western medicine.

Simultaneously, traditional medicine systems, such as Traditional Chinese Medicine and Ayurveda, continued to thrive and evolve. The Portuguese and Dutch traders in Asia played a pivotal role in the dissemination of Asian herbal knowledge, introducing herbs like ginseng and turmeric to Europe.

Scientific Advances and Modern Herbal Medicine

The 19th and 20th centuries witnessed a scientific revolution that transformed the way herbal medicine was studied and utilized. The isolation and identification of active chemical compounds from plants led to the development of synthetic drugs and the rise of modern pharmacology. As a result, traditional herbal remedies experienced a decline in popularity.

However, the integration of science and traditional practices in the late 20th century sparked a resurgence of interest in herbal medicine. Herbalists and scientists began to collaborate, conducting research on the efficacy and safety of medicinal plants. This renewed interest led to the standardization and commercialization of herbal products, resulting in the establishment of regulatory bodies to ensure their quality and safety.

Traditional herbal knowledge from different cultures continues to be explored by modern researchers. For example, the discovery of the anti-malarial properties of artemisinin in Artemisia annua, a Chinese medicinal herb, exemplifies how ancient wisdom can still hold immense value in the search for effective treatments.

The evolution of herbal knowledge is a testament to the wisdom and ingenuity of humankind. From the ancient civilizations to the present day, herbal medicine has played an essential role in healthcare systems worldwide. The integration of traditional practices and modern scientific approaches continues to shape the field, as researchers strive to uncover the full potential of medicinal plants. By recognizing and respecting the diverse herbal traditions that have been passed down through generations, we can harness their powers to improve health and well-being for future generations.

Chapter 2: Botanical Diversity and Identification

When observing the natural world, one cannot help but be captivated by the vast array of plant species that exist. From towering trees to delicate flowers, plants have evolved into an astonishing diversity of forms and functions. In this chapter, we will explore the wonders of botanical diversity and delve into the intricate processes involved in the identification of plant species. By the end of this chapter, readers will have gained a deeper appreciation for the complexity and beauty of the plant kingdom.

Section 1: The Importance of Botanical Diversity

1.1 Ecosystem Stability:

Botanical diversity plays a vital role in maintaining the stability and resilience of ecosystems. Each plant species has its unique set of adaptations, allowing it to occupy a particular niche within its environment. By filling various ecological roles, plants ensure the efficient cycling of nutrients, promote soil health, and provide habitat and food resources for a multitude of other organisms. The loss of even a single plant species can have far-reaching consequences, potentially causing disruptions in entire ecosystems.

1.2 Human Well-being:

Beyond their ecological significance, plants contribute fundamentally to human well-being. They provide us with essential resources such as food, medicine, and shelter. A diverse array of crops, including grains, fruits, and vegetables, sustain our growing population. Medicines derived from plants are indispensable in treating various diseases, and plant-based fibers are utilized in the production of clothing and building materials. Appreciating the value of botanical diversity is thus crucial for ensuring the sustainability of our planet and our own survival.

Section 2: Exploring Botanical Diversity

2.1 Taxonomy: The Science of Classification:

In order to understand and study botanical diversity, we rely on a system of classification called taxonomy. Developed by Swedish botanist Carl Linnaeus in the eighteenth century, taxonomy aims to categorize and organize plant species based on their evolutionary relationships. By assigning each plant a unique scientific name, taxonomy allows scientists to communicate effectively and avoid confusion. The hierarchy of plant classification ranges from the broadest level, the kingdom, to increasingly specific categories including phylum, class, order, family, genus, and species.

2.2 Major Plant Groups:

The study of botanical diversity introduces us to a wide range of plant groups, each with its distinctive characteristics. We will briefly explore some of the notable plant groups here:

2.2.1 Bryophytes:

Bryophytes, including mosses, liverworts, and hornworts, are among the most ancient land plants. These small, non-vascular plants lack true roots, stems, and leaves. Bryophytes often colonize moist environments, playing vital roles in preventing soil erosion and acting as indicators of water and air quality.

2.2.2 Ferns and Fern Allies:

Ferns and their allies, like horsetails and clubmosses, represent another fascinating group of plants. These spore-bearing plants originated during the Carboniferous period and quickly diversified. Ferns are characterized by their feathery fronds, while horsetails possess jointed, hollow stems. These plants reproduce through spores rather than seeds and are dominant in a variety of habitats, ranging from tropical rainforests to arctic tundras.

2.2.3 Conifers:

Conifers, which include pine, spruce, and cedar, are gymnosperms - seed-bearing plants that first appeared during the late Carboniferous period. Easily recognizable by their needle-like or scale-like leaves, conifers are adapted to temperate and cold environments and often dominate boreal forests. Many conifer species produce valuable timber and are crucial in maintaining the balance of global carbon cycles.

2.2.4 Flowering Plants:

Flowering plants, known as angiosperms, represent the most diverse and abundant group of plants on Earth. Having evolved around 140 million years ago, angiosperms boast a wide variety of forms, from towering trees like oaks and maples to delicate wildflowers. Their flowers have played a significant role in attracting pollinators, enabling successful sexual reproduction. The diversity of angiosperms is staggering, comprising numerous families such as the daisy family (Asteraceae), the orchid family (Orchidaceae), and the grass family (Poaceae).

Section 3: Plant Identification Methods

3.1 Morphological Characteristics:

One of the primary methods used to identify plants is through the examination of their morphological characteristics. These can include leaf shape, size, and arrangement, flower structure, bark texture, and growth habit. By comparing these traits to botanical keys or field guides, botanists can often determine the identity of a particular plant species.

3.2 Molecular Techniques:

In addition to morphological characteristics, advances in molecular biology have revolutionized the field of plant identification. Techniques such as DNA barcoding allow scientists to compare and analyze specific DNA regions unique to each plant species. By sequencing and comparing these regions, plants can be accurately identified even when their usual identifying features are absent or difficult to distinguish.

Section 4: Challenges and Future Directions

4.1 Preservation of Botanical Diversity:

The preservation of botanical diversity poses significant challenges in the face of deforestation, habitat destruction, and climate change. It is crucial that we prioritize the conservation of plant species and their habitats through the establishment of protected areas, reforestation efforts, and sustainable land management practices. Additionally, fostering public awareness and education about the value of plants can encourage actions that support their conservation.

4.2 The Role of Technology:

Technology continues to play an increasingly important role in understanding and documenting botanical diversity. Advances in imaging techniques, remote sensing, and data analysis enable scientists to explore and monitor plant populations in ways that were previously impossible. This integration of technology with traditional identification methods holds great promise for enhancing our understanding of botanical diversity and accelerating the discovery of new plant species.

In this chapter, we have embarked on a journey through the captivating world of botanical diversity and identification. We have witnessed the essential role that plants play in maintaining ecosystem stability and supporting human well-being. By exploring the major plant groups and delving into the methods used to identify them, we have unlocked the potential for a deeper understanding of the natural world. As we continue to explore the wonders of botany, it is crucial that we work tirelessly to preserve and appreciate the astonishing diversity of plant life that surrounds us.

Exploring Plant Varieties and Species

Plants are at the very core of Earth's diverse ecosystems. They provide oxygen, food, medicine, and shelter to countless organisms, including humans. The sheer beauty and complexity of plant life has intrigued botanists and nature enthusiasts for centuries.

In this chapter, we will embark on an exciting journey of exploring the vast world of plant varieties and species. We will delve into the remarkable adaptations that plants have developed to thrive in different environments, uncover the interconnectedness of plant species, and celebrate the incredible diversity that exists in the plant kingdom.

Understanding Plant Varieties:

When we think of plants, we often imagine towering trees, colorful flowers, or lush green grass. However, plants encompass a much broader range of organisms. Whether they are microscopic algae floating in a pond or mosses covering a forest floor, plants come in an astonishing array of shapes, sizes, and forms.

Plants can be classified into different varieties based on their life cycles, growth habits, and physical characteristics. Annual plants complete their life cycle within a year, while perennial plants survive for multiple years. Herbs are non-woody plants with soft stems, while shrubs and trees have woody stems and grow taller.

Within each variety, there are numerous species. Species are groups of plants that share similar traits and can interbreed to produce fertile offspring. To date, scientists have identified over 300,000 plant species, and new discoveries continue to be made. Each species has its unique set of characteristics, making the exploration of plant species an awe-inspiring endeavor.

Plant Adaptations:

Plants have evolved diverse adaptations to survive in different environments. These adaptations allow them to withstand harsh climate conditions, compete for resources, and interact with other organisms. Let's take a closer look at some fascinating plant adaptations.

One common adaptation is the presence of roots. Roots anchor plants in the ground and absorb water and nutrients from the soil. Some plants have specialized roots, such as prop roots in mangroves or pneumatophores in swamp-dwelling trees, which help them cope with waterlogged environments.

Another crucial adaptation is photosynthesis. Most plants use chlorophyll and sunlight to convert carbon dioxide and water into glucose, a form of stored energy. However, in some extreme environments, such as deserts or tundra, where water is scarce or temperatures are extremely low, plants have developed alternative photosynthetic paths, like CAM or C4 photosynthesis.

Furthermore, plants have evolved various reproductive strategies. Some plants rely on insects or birds for pollination, while others utilize wind or water to disperse their pollen. The incredible diversity of plant reproductive structures, including eye-catching flowers or intricately shaped cones, showcases the evolutionary adaptations that have occurred over millions of years.

Interconnectedness of Plant Species:

While each plant species has its unique characteristics, they are all connected within intricate webs of ecological interactions. Plants rely on other organisms, such as animals and microbes, for their survival and reproduction. In turn, they provide resources and services to these organisms, forming complex relationships.

Insects, for example, play a crucial role in plant pollination. Bees, butterflies, and other insects transfer pollen from one flower to another, facilitating plant reproduction. This symbiotic relationship benefits both the pollinators, who receive nectar or pollen as food, and the plants, who are ensured successful pollination.

Similarly, many animals depend on plants for food and shelter. Herbivores, like deer or cows, feed on plant leaves or grass, while frugivores, such as birds or monkeys, rely on fruits for nourishment. The intricate balance between plants and animals shapes entire ecosystems and highlights the interconnectedness of all living organisms.

Plant Exploration:

Plant exploration has been a vital component of scientific discovery for centuries. Early explorers ventured into unknown territories, collecting plant specimens that not only provided invaluable scientific knowledge but also paved the way for advances in medicine, agriculture, and horticulture.

One famous plant explorer was Sir Joseph Banks, a botanist who accompanied Captain James Cook on his voyages in the 18th century. Banks collected a vast number of plants from different continents, introducing several species to Europe, such as eucalyptus or acacia. These plant explorations transformed horticulture and expanded our understanding of plant diversity worldwide.

Today, plant exploration continues with dedicated individuals, research institutions, and botanical gardens. Botanists and ecologists venture into remote regions, including rainforests, deserts, or mountains, to document and collect plant specimens. These collections provide valuable insights into plant diversity, distribution, and potential uses, aiding conservation efforts and enhancing our understanding of the natural world.

Exploring plant varieties and species is an endless journey of wonder and discovery. From tiny mosses to towering trees, plants have colonized the Earth in remarkable ways.

Their adaptations, reproductive strategies, and ecological interconnectedness paint a vivid picture of the incredible diversity and resilience of life on our planet.

Understanding plant varieties and species is not only essential for scientific inquiry but also for our well-being. Plants provide us with sustenance, serve as sources of medicine, and offer us solace in the beauty of their existence.

By valuing and preserving plant diversity, we can ensure a more sustainable and vibrant future for generations to come.

Fundamentals of Botanical Classification

Botanical classification is a systematic method used to categorize plant species based on their shared characteristics. This classification system plays a crucial role in the field of botany, allowing scientists to organize and understand the vast diversity of plant species found across the globe. In this chapter, we will explore the fundamentals of botanical classification, the various classification systems used, and the significance of this discipline in our understanding of plant life.

The Need for Classification

With an estimated 390,000 known plant species on Earth, the need for a classification system becomes apparent. Imagine a world without an organized means of identifying and studying plants – it would be a chaotic jumble of diverse species without any clear connections or patterns. Botanical classification provides us with a framework for organizing this immense diversity into manageable groups, facilitating our comprehension of plant life and enabling effective communication among researchers and enthusiasts.

Taxonomy: The Foundation of Botanical Classification

At the heart of botanical classification lies the science of taxonomy.

Developed by the Swedish botanist Carl Linnaeus in the 18th century, taxonomy provides the rules and principles for organizing and naming plants. The fundamental unit of plant classification is the species, which is defined as a group of organisms that share common characteristics and can interbreed to produce fertile offspring.

Taxonomists employ a hierarchical system that begins with the broadest category – the kingdom – and gradually narrows down to the most specific category – the genus and species. Currently, plant taxonomy recognizes five kingdoms: Monera, Protista, Fungi, Plantae, and Animalia. Within the kingdom Plantae, the classification continues from division to class, order, family, genus, and, finally, species. This hierarchical approach provides a logical structure and allows for finer distinctions between closely related plants.

The Importance of Morphological Characteristics

To classify plants accurately, botanists rely heavily on morphological characteristics – the physical traits that plants exhibit. These features can be observed in various plant parts, such as leaves, stems, flowers, fruits, and roots. By studying morphological characteristics, taxonomists can group plants based on similarities and differences in structure, function, and appearance.

Let's consider an example: the rose family (Rosaceae). This plant family is characterized by several distinctive morphological features, including alternate leaves, five-petaled flowers, and a fruit called a pome. These shared characteristics allow botanists to classify various species within the rose family, such as roses (Rosa), apples (Malus), and strawberries (Fragaria), into a common taxonomic group.

Limitations of Morphological Classification

While morphological characteristics are valuable for plant identification, they have their limitations. Morphological traits can vary within a plant species due to environmental factors, making classification solely based on appearance challenging. Additionally, some plant species may exhibit convergent evolution – where unrelated plants evolve similar characteristics due to similar environmental pressures – further complicating classification based solely on morphology.

Advancements in Molecular Classification

To overcome the limitations of morphology-based classification and achieve more accurate taxonomic relationships, scientists have turned to molecular techniques in recent decades. Molecular classification involves analyzing the genetic material (DNA or RNA) of plants to determine their relatedness. By comparing specific genetic markers, such as gene sequences or DNA fingerprints, scientists can create phylogenetic trees that illustrate the evolutionary relationships among different plant species.

One notable molecular classification technique is DNA barcoding, which uses specific gene sequences to identify and classify plants. This technique relies on a section of DNA that is highly conserved within a species but varies between species. By comparing these

DNA sequences, taxonomists can quickly identify and classify plants, even when morphology alone proves insufficient.

The Role of Botanical Classification in Conservation

Botanical classification is not merely an academic exercise; it serves crucial practical purposes as well. A comprehensive understanding of plant taxonomy helps identify plant species that are endangered, rare, or threatened. This knowledge is invaluable for conservation efforts, allowing scientists to prioritize species for protection and develop effective strategies to prevent their extinction.

Moreover, accurate botanical classification assists in documenting global plant diversity, understanding plant evolution, and identifying potential medicinal plants. By recognizing the relationships between different plant groups, scientists can also predict the characteristics and potential uses of poorly studied species based on their classification within a known group.

In Botanical Classification, we have explored the fundamentals of this essential discipline in botany. From taxonomy and the hierarchical classification system to morphological characteristics, molecular techniques, and the practical applications, this chapter has provided insight into the diverse tools and approaches employed in botanical classification. By organizing and understanding plant species, we can further our knowledge of plant life, contribute to conservation efforts, and unlock the countless marvels hidden within the botanical realm.

Tools for Proper Plant Identification

Plant identification is a fascinating and essential skill for botanists, horticulturists, gardeners, and nature enthusiasts alike. Being able to correctly identify plant species not only enhances our understanding of the natural world but also allows us to make informed decisions about plant management, conservation efforts, and even the creation of aesthetically pleasing gardens.

In the past, plant identification often relied on the knowledge and experience of experts. However, with advancements in technology and the availability of reliable resources, amateur plant enthusiasts can now take on the challenge of plant identification with confidence. In this chapter, we will explore the various tools available for proper plant identification and how they can be effectively used.

Field Guides:

Field guides have long been a staple tool for plant identification enthusiasts. These comprehensive books contain detailed descriptions, photographs, and illustrations of various plant species, allowing users to compare observed characteristics with those presented in the guide. Field guides are typically organized by families, genera, or habitats, making them suitable for different levels of expertise.

When using a field guide, it is essential to consider its relevance to your geographical region, as some guides may focus on specific areas or have limited coverage. Additionally, field guides can quickly become outdated as new species are discovered or taxonomy is revised. Therefore, it is advisable to choose the most up-to-date edition available.

Online Databases and Apps:

With the ever-growing accessibility of the internet, online databases and apps have revolutionized plant identification. These digital tools provide instant access to a vast amount of information, allowing users to search for plant species using various criteria, such as appearance, habitat, and geographical location.

One popular online database is the USDA Plants Database, which contains a wealth of information about plants native to the United States and its territories. Users can search for specific species or browse through various categories, including trees, wildflowers, and grasses. The database provides detailed descriptions, photographs, distribution maps, and even information on their ecological significance and cultural uses.

Mobile applications, such as PlantSnap and iNaturalist, offer similar functionalities but with the convenience of being accessible on smartphones and tablets. These apps utilize artificial intelligence and crowdsourcing to identify plants based on uploaded photos. They often provide instant results, community feedback, and even suggestions for related species.

Microscopy:

For more advanced plant identification, the use of microscopy can be invaluable. Microscopes allow users to observe minute details of a plant's structure, including leaf and stem anatomy, pollen, and seed characteristics. These details are often crucial in distinguishing between closely related species or identifying plant parts that may be challenging to ascertain with the naked eye.

When utilizing microscopy, it is essential to have a basic understanding of the plant's anatomy and be familiar with various techniques for preparing and staining plant samples. Additionally, access to an appropriate microscope with sufficient magnification capabilities is necessary for accurate observation.

Herbarium Specimens:

Herbarium specimens are dried plant specimens that have been preserved and stored in botanical collections. These specimens serve as a valuable resource for plant identification, as they provide a physical record of a plant's characteristics at a specific point in time. Herbarium collections are often associated with botanical gardens, research institutes, or universities and can contain millions of specimens from around the world.

Public herbarium collections often offer access to their specimens for research purposes, either physically or through digital repositories. Users can request to examine or photograph specimens or explore the collection's online databases, which provide detailed information about each specimen, including taxonomic identification, locality, and collector's name.

DNA Barcoding:

In recent years, DNA barcoding has emerged as a powerful tool for plant identification. This technique utilizes short DNA sequences, typically from specific genes, as a unique identifier for a particular species. By comparing an unknown plant's DNA sequence to a comprehensive database, researchers can determine its species identity accurately.

DNA barcoding offers several advantages over traditional identification methods. It can be used on various plant parts, including leaves, flowers, or even degraded samples, making it applicable in situations where other features may not be accessible. Additionally, DNA barcoding has the potential to identify cryptic or morphologically similar species that can be challenging to differentiate by traditional means.

However, it is important to note that DNA barcoding generally requires specialized laboratory equipment and expertise, making it less accessible to the average plant enthusiast. Nonetheless, as the technology becomes more widespread, we can expect DNA barcoding to play an increasingly significant role in plant identification.

The tools discussed in this chapter represent a diverse range of options available for proper plant identification. Whether you are a novice or an experienced botanist, there is a tool suited to your level of expertise and available resources. From field guides and online databases to microscopy, herbarium specimens, and DNA barcoding, each tool offers unique advantages and enriches our understanding of plant diversity.

As you embark on your journey into the world of plant identification, it is important to remember that no single tool can provide definitive identification in all scenarios. It often necessitates combining multiple tools or consulting with experts to ensure accurate species identification. Embrace the adventure of discovering and unraveling the mysteries of plant life, and may these tools help you on your path to becoming a proficient plant identifier.

Sustainable Harvesting and Cultivation

In our quest for economic progress and development, we must not overlook the importance of sustainable practices in the realm of natural resource utilization. Human activities, particularly in the fields of agriculture, forestry, and fisheries, have exerted immense pressure on ecosystems and threatened biodiversity, all while jeopardizing the long-term availability of vital resources. Therefore, it becomes imperative to adopt a more mindful and responsible approach towards harvesting and cultivation. This chapter delves into the concept of sustainable harvesting and cultivation, exploring its fundamental principles, various techniques, benefits, and challenges we face in implementing these practices.

Defining Sustainable Harvesting and Cultivation:

Sustainable harvesting and cultivation encompass a set of principles and practices that aim to meet current resource needs without compromising the ability of future generations to meet their own needs. It involves striking a delicate balance between exploiting natural resources and ensuring their regeneration, while minimizing negative impact on the environment and fostering community well-being.

Principles of Sustainable Harvesting and Cultivation:

1. Ecosystem-Based Approach: Sustainable practices necessitate the understanding that ecosystems are interconnected and dynamic, and must be managed as a whole. Recognizing the intricate web of relationships among different species, habitats, and ecosystems is essential to avoid depleting resources and causing irreparable damage.

2. Biodiversity Conservation: Conserving and promoting biodiversity is a cornerstone of sustainable harvesting and cultivation. By preserving genetic diversity and the resilience of ecosystems, we enhance their capacity to adapt to changing conditions and maintain ecological balance.

3. Effective Governance and Management: Sustainable resource management requires effective governance, encompassing policies, regulations, and institutions that prioritize social, economic, and environmental concerns. Empowering local communities with participatory decision-making can generate buy-in and foster responsible approaches to harvesting and cultivation.

Techniques for Sustainable Harvesting and Cultivation:
1. Organic Farming: Conventional farming often relies on the heavy use of synthetic inputs such as chemical fertilizers and pesticides, which can have adverse effects on ecosystems, soil health, and human health. Organic farming, on the other hand, adopts practices that minimize environmental impact, promote soil fertility, and

prioritize natural pest control. By avoiding the use of synthetic chemicals, organic farming enhances food quality, reduces pollution, and supports biodiversity.

2. Agroforestry: Agroforestry integrates trees with agricultural practices, diversifying landscapes, and harnessing multiple benefits. Trees provide shade, shelter, and habitat for beneficial insects and animals, while increasing soil fertility and sequestering carbon. Combining crops and trees in the same area enhances productivity, fosters resource conservation, and improves resilience to climate change.

3. Selective Logging: Unsustainable logging practices have been a major driver of deforestation and ecosystem degradation. Selective logging involves the careful removal of individual trees, considering their size, species, and ecological role. By avoiding clear-cutting and allowing natural regeneration, selective logging minimizes soil erosion, retains habitat for wildlife, and maintains the integrity of forest ecosystems.

Benefits of Sustainable Harvesting and Cultivation:

1. Environmental Preservation: Adopting sustainable practices mitigates environmental degradation, conserves biodiversity, and helps protect fragile ecosystems. By safeguarding habitats and minimizing pollution, we can safeguard valuable resources for future generations.

2. Economic Opportunities: Sustainable harvesting and cultivation methods can generate economic benefits in various sectors. For instance, organic farming offers premium prices for produce, while eco-tourism and sustainable fisheries create employment opportunities and support local economies. By embracing

environmentally friendly practices, communities can cultivate economic resilience and foster sustainable livelihoods.

3. Climate Change Mitigation: Sustainable practices play a crucial role in mitigating the effects of climate change. Agroforestry and sustainable forestry methods sequester carbon and contribute to reducing greenhouse gas emissions. By embracing practices that reduce reliance on fossil fuels, such as organic farming and renewable energy sources, we can make significant progress towards a low-carbon future.

Challenges and Future Directions:

Implementing sustainable harvesting and cultivation practices is not without its challenges. The shift often requires investment, technical expertise, and a change in mindset. Overcoming these hurdles should involve collaboration among governments, businesses, and local communities. Nevertheless, the potential rewards are worth the effort.

In the face of a growing global population and growing environmental concerns, sustainable harvesting and cultivation remain imperative. By adopting these practices, we can secure our natural resources, protect biodiversity, and build resilient communities. This chapter aimed to shed light on the fundamental principles, techniques, benefits, and challenges associated with sustainable harvesting and cultivation. It is essential for all stakeholders to unite in taking decisive action that preserves our planet's resources for generations to come.

Chapter 3: Principles of Herbal Preparation

Herbal medicine has been used for centuries as a natural alternative to conventional medicine. The effectiveness and safety of herbal remedies lie in the way they are prepared and administered. In this chapter, we will explore the principles of herbal preparation, including the methods of extraction, dosage forms, and considerations for proper storage. Understanding these principles is crucial for anyone seeking to harness the healing power of herbs.

Methods of Extraction

1. Infusion

An infusion involves steeping herbs in hot water to extract their active constituents. This method is suitable for delicate plant parts such as flowers, leaves, and aromatic herbs. To prepare an infusion, follow these steps:

a. Boil water and pour it over the herbs in a heat-resistant container.
b. Cover the container, allowing the herbs to steep for 15-20 minutes.
c. Strain the infusion through a fine mesh sieve or muslin cloth, separating the liquid from the plant material.
d. The resulting liquid can be consumed as a beverage or used externally, depending on its intended purpose.

2. Decoction

In contrast to infusions, decoctions are used to extract active constituents from tougher plant parts like roots, barks, and seeds. The process involves boiling the herbs to release their medicinal properties. The steps for preparing a decoction are as follows:

a. Place the herbs in a pot and add cold water.
b. Slowly bring the water to a boil and let it simmer for 30-60 minutes.
c. Allow the decoction to cool and strain out the plant material.
d. The resulting liquid can be consumed or used externally.

3. Tinctures

Tinctures are concentrated liquid extracts of herbs. They are made by dissolving the medicinal constituents of the plant in alcohol, vinegar, or glycerin. Tinctures offer long shelf life and increased potency due to their extraction method. Here's how to make a tincture:

a. Chop or grind the herb finely.
b. Fill a glass jar with the herb, leaving some space at the top. Ensure the herb is completely covered but not overly soaked in the solvent.
c. Seal the jar tightly and allow it to sit in a cool, dark place for several weeks or even months, shaking it periodically.
d. After the desired extraction period, strain the liquid through a

cheesecloth or fine mesh sieve, squeezing out as much liquid as possible.

e. Store the resulting tincture in glass amber bottles away from direct sunlight.

4. Maceration

Similar to tinctures, maceration involves extracting plant constituents in a liquid solvent, but without the need for alcohol. Maceration is particularly useful when preparing herbal remedies for children or individuals who avoid alcohol. The process goes as follows:

a. Finely chop or grind the plant material.

b. Fill a glass jar with the herb, covering it completely with an appropriate solvent, such as vegetable oil or water.

c. Seal the jar tightly and leave it to sit for a few weeks, occasionally shaking the jar.

d. After the desired extraction period, strain the liquid and store it in a dark amber bottle.

Dosage Forms

1. Herbal Teas

Herbal teas are perhaps the most common dosage form of herbal preparations. Infusions and decoctions can be consumed as hot or cold teas. Besides their therapeutic effects, herbal teas provide a comforting and enjoyable experience. The dosage for herbal teas varies depending on the herb, its strength, and the desired effect. One to two cups per day is generally recommended, although this may increase under the guidance of a qualified herbalist.

2. Capsules and Tablets

For those who prefer a more convenient dosage form, capsules and tablets provide a practical solution. Herbal extracts or powders are encapsulated or compressed into easy-to-swallow pills. These dosage forms are desirable when taste or portability is a concern. However, it is important to consult with a healthcare professional to determine the appropriate dosage for a given herb or blend.

3. Topical Preparations

Some herbs are best applied externally to address various skin conditions, wounds, or muscle strains. Infused oils, ointments, creams, and poultices are effective ways of delivering herbal benefits directly to the affected area. For example, comfrey and calendula oil can be used topically to promote wound healing, while arnica gel aids in relieving muscle soreness.

Considerations for Proper Storage

To maintain the potency and effectiveness of herbal preparations, proper storage is essential. Follow these guidelines for prolonged shelf life:

1. Store herbs in airtight containers, preferably made of dark-colored glass, to protect them from light, heat, and moisture.

2. Keep containers in a cool, dry place away from direct sunlight.

3. Label each container with the herb's name, preparation date, and dosage instructions.

4. Discard any herbs that show signs of mold, discoloration, or an unpleasant odor.

Understanding the principles of herbal preparation is essential for safely and effectively utilizing the healing power of herbs. From extraction methods to dosage forms and storage considerations, each step plays a crucial role in maximizing the efficacy of herbal remedies. By following these principles, individuals can harness the full potential of herbal medicine as a natural and holistic approach to health and well-being.

Harvesting and Collecting Medicinal Plants

The use of medicinal plants for healing and wellness has been a part of human civilization for centuries. The power of nature's remedies has captivated healers and practitioners worldwide, and even today, medicinal plants continue to play a crucial role in traditional and modern medicine. However, proper harvesting and collecting techniques are vital to ensure the sustainability of these plants while maximizing their therapeutic benefits. In this chapter, we will delve into the art and science of harvesting and collecting medicinal plants, exploring the best practices to preserve their potency and promote ecological balance.

Understanding Medicinal Plants:

Before delving into the techniques of harvesting and collecting medicinal plants, it is essential to develop a deep understanding of these remarkable organisms. Medicinal plants are a diverse group of flora, comprising herbs, trees, shrubs, and even certain fungi. Each plant species possesses unique chemical compounds that contribute to its healing properties. These compounds, known as secondary metabolites, include alkaloids, flavonoids, terpenes, and more. The concentration and stability of these compounds vary throughout the plant's lifecycle, emphasizing the importance of proper harvesting methods.

Sustainable Harvesting:

Sustainable harvesting practices are crucial to ensure the long-term availability of medicinal plants. Overharvesting can drive certain species towards extinction, disrupt ecosystems, and compromise the collective health of our planet. As responsible stewards of medicinal plants, we must adhere to the following principles:

1. Respect local regulations: Familiarize yourself with local laws and regulations surrounding the harvesting and collecting of medicinal plants. These guidelines often restrict the collection of endangered species, specify quotas, and establish appropriate seasons or growth stages for harvesting.

2. Understand plant life cycles: To minimize ecological impact, learn about the life cycle of each medicinal plant species you plan to harvest. Understanding the plant's growth patterns, flowering times, and seed dispersal mechanisms will enable you to harvest at the right stage without negatively affecting its ability to reproduce.

3. Adopt selective harvesting: Instead of uprooting or entirely removing the plant, practice selective harvesting. Focus on the parts that hold the highest medicinal value, such as leaves, flowers, or roots. By leaving a significant portion intact, you allow the plant to regenerate and continue its vital ecological functions.

4. Monitor collection quantities: Keep track of how much you collect and assess the impact of your harvest over time. This information will enable you to adjust your collection practices accordingly and

maintain a sustainable balance between human needs and ecological preservation.

Harvesting Techniques:

Now that we have established the importance of sustainability, let us explore some practical techniques for harvesting medicinal plants effectively:

1. Timing: Timing is crucial when harvesting medicinal plants. In general, gather the plant material during its peak potency season. Researchers, ethnobotanists, and traditional healers often offer valuable insights into the optimal time based on historical practices and observational knowledge.

2. Tools: Ensure you have the appropriate tools for harvesting, such as sharp pruning shears, scissors, or a sharp knife. These tools should be clean and sterile to prevent the transmission of diseases or contamination between plants.

3. Handling: Handle the plants gently to minimize damage and degradation of their medicinal properties. Avoid bruising, crushing, or damaging the parts you are harvesting. Moisture-sensitive plant materials can be harvested during dry weather to maintain their integrity.

4. Proper storage: Once harvested, store the plant material properly to maintain its quality. Most medicinal plants benefit from drying, a method that removes excess moisture without compromising active

compounds. Use well-ventilated drying racks, drying sheds, or dehydrators, ensuring the temperature remains low to prevent degradation.

Ecological Considerations:

Beyond the sustainability and technical aspects of harvesting medicinal plants, it is vital to cultivate an awareness of the broader ecological implications. Understanding the interconnections within ecosystems can foster respectful and reciprocal relationships between humans and the natural world:

1. Native species preservation: Whenever possible, prioritize harvesting native medicinal plants. These species have adapted to local ecological conditions and often play a vital role in maintaining biodiversity. By focusing on native plants, we contribute to the preservation of traditional knowledge, local ecosystems, and the cultural heritage connected to these plants.

2. Cultivation and propagation: To reduce pressure on wild populations, consider cultivating medicinal plants in a garden or greenhouse. This practice ensures a sustainable source of supply while protecting wild populations from overharvesting. Furthermore, germinating and propagating seeds or cuttings can provide an opportunity to increase the availability of rare or endangered medicinal plants.

3. Ecosystem stewardship: Expanding our roles as stewards of medicinal plants involves actively participating in ecological

conservation efforts. Contributing to habitat restoration, supporting local conservation organizations, and spreading awareness about the importance of preserving natural areas are essential steps towards creating a more sustainable future.

Harvesting and collecting medicinal plants is both an art and a science. It requires deep respect for nature, a comprehensive understanding of plant species, and the implementation of sustainable practices.

By following proper harvesting techniques, respecting regulatory frameworks, and nurturing ecological awareness, we can ensure the longevity of medicinal plants while harnessing their extraordinary healing powers for generations to come.

Drying, Storing, and Preserving Herbs

Herbs have been a staple in human society for centuries, revered not only for their culinary uses but also for their medicinal properties and aromatic qualities. However, their delicate nature means that they cannot be stored for extended periods without undergoing some form of preservation. In this chapter, we will explore the various methods of drying, storing, and preserving herbs, enabling you to enjoy their flavors and benefits all year round.

Section 1: Harvesting Herbs

Before we delve into the different preservation techniques, it is essential to understand when and how best to harvest your herbs. The ideal time to gather most herbs is in the morning, just after the dew has evaporated, but before the heat of the day sets in. Select leaves that appear healthy, free from pests, and have not yet flowered to ensure optimal flavor and potency.

Section 2: Drying Herbs

Drying herbs is one of the most common methods of preservation, as it helps lock in their flavors and extends their shelf life. There are several techniques for drying herbs, including air drying, oven drying, and using a dehydrator.

2.1 Air Drying:

Air drying is the traditional method of drying herbs and requires minimal equipment. Start by bundling 5-10 stems of herbs together using a string or rubber band and hang them upside down in a cool, dark, and ventilated area. Ensure that each bundle is not too large to ensure proper airflow. Herbs such as rosemary, sage, thyme, and oregano are particularly suited for air drying.

2.2 Oven Drying:

If you are short on time or live in a humid climate, oven drying is a viable alternative. Begin by preheating your oven to the lowest setting (around 100-115°F or 40-45°C). Remove the individual herb leaves from their stems and spread them in a single layer on a baking sheet. Place the sheet in the oven, leaving the door slightly ajar to allow for airflow. Regularly check on the herbs and rotate the tray as needed to ensure even drying.

2.3 Dehydrating:

Investing in a food dehydrator is another excellent option for drying herbs. This device allows for precise temperature control and airflow, resulting in consistent and efficient drying. Follow the manufacturer's instructions for the specific herbs you are drying, as temperature and drying times may vary slightly.

Section 3: Storing Dried Herbs

Once your herbs are completely dry, it's crucial to store them properly to maintain their flavor and potency.

3.1 Choosing Storage Containers:

Select airtight containers, such as glass jars with tight-fitting lids or resealable bags, to prevent moisture and air from degrading the herbs. Avoid using plastic containers, as they can react with the herbs, altering their flavor. Additionally, ensure that the chosen containers are thoroughly clean and dry before adding the dried herbs.

3.2 Proper Labeling:

Label each container with the name of the herb, its harvest date, and any other pertinent information. This will help you keep track of their freshness and usage.

3.3 Storage Location:

Store your dried herbs in a cool, dark, and dry place to retain their quality. Avoid storing them near windows or other sources of light, as prolonged exposure can lead to color and flavor degradation.

3.4 Shelf Life:

Though dried herbs generally maintain their flavor for up to a year, it is advisable to replenish your stock annually to ensure maximum freshness and potency.

Section 4: Other Methods of Preserving Herbs

While drying herbs is the most popular preservation method, other techniques allow you to savor their flavors and medicinal properties in alternative ways.

4.1 Freezing:

Freezing herbs is an excellent method for retaining flavors and is particularly useful for herbs with high water content, such as basil and parsley. After washing and drying the herbs thoroughly, chop them finely or leave them as whole leaves and transfer them into ice cube trays. Fill each compartment with water or olive oil, cover, and freeze. Once frozen, transfer the herb cubes to resealable bags or airtight containers for long-term storage.

4.2 Herbal Infused Oils and Vinegars:

Infusing oils or vinegars with herbs provides an exciting way to incorporate their flavors into everyday cooking. Simply fill a glass jar with a variety of herbs, ensuring they are completely dry, and cover them with either olive oil or vinegar. Secure the lid tightly and store the jar in a cool, dark place for several weeks, occasionally shaking it to distribute the flavors. Strain the mixture, and you'll be left with a delicious herb-infused oil or vinegar to enhance your culinary creations.

4.3 Herb Salt or Sugar:

Creating herb-infused salt or sugar is an innovative method that not only preserves your herbs but also adds a unique twist to your dishes. To make herb salt, finely chop your chosen herbs and mix them with an equal amount of salt. Store this mixture in an airtight container, allowing the flavors to meld together for a few weeks. For herb sugar, follow the same process but substitute sugar for the salt. Both herb salt and sugar can be used to season various dishes or as a decorative touch for desserts.

Drying, storing, and preserving herbs are essential skills for every herb enthusiast. By carefully selecting the appropriate preservation method and following guidelines for harvesting and storage, you can enjoy the flavors, aromas, and medicinal benefits of herbs year-round. So, why not embark on your herb preservation journey and create a pantry filled with fragrant and flavorful possibilities?

Extraction Methods: Infusions, Decoctions, Tinctures

In the world of herbal medicine, the extraction of active compounds from plants is a fundamental practice. The knowledge and techniques of extracting these beneficial constituents have been passed down through generations, enabling healers to harness the power of nature. This chapter delves into the three primary methods of extraction: infusions, decoctions, and tinctures. Each method holds its own unique properties and benefits, ensuring holistic healing practices. So, let us embark on a journey through the intricate world of extraction methods.

Section 1: Infusions

1.1 What is an Infusion?

Infusion is one of the oldest and simplest extraction methods known to mankind. It involves extracting medicinal properties from herbs by soaking them in hot or cold water. The heat helps dissolve the active constituents, resulting in a potent herbal brew. The process is akin to making tea, although infusions often require longer steeping times for more substantial extraction.

1.2 The Art of Infusion

To prepare an infusion, start by selecting high-quality herbs or plant materials suited for your intended application. Dried herbs tend to work best, as excess water content can dilute the potency. However, some fresh herbs can also be infused, especially those with high water content, like mints and citruses.

Next, consider the time and temperature needed for the infusion. Delicate herbs such as flowers and leaves require lower temperatures, while hardy roots and barks may need hotter water to extract their therapeutic compounds fully. Boiling water is typically used for roots, barks, and seeds, while simmering water suffices for most other herbal materials.

1.3 Benefits and Applications

Infusions offer a versatile way of extracting a wide range of compounds from plants. They are an excellent method for extracting essential oils, polyphenols, alkaloids, and other water-soluble constituents. Infusions are commonly used for digestive remedies, teas, soothing skin tonics, and herbal baths.

Herbal teas, a popular example of infusion, provide a way to consume various plants' medicinal qualities. For instance, chamomile infusions are renowned for their relaxation properties, while peppermint infusions aid digestion and ease discomfort. The possibilities are endless when it comes to crafting custom infusions to address specific health concerns.

Section 2: Decoctions

2.1 What is a Decoction?

Decoction is a slightly more complex extraction method that involves simmering plant material in water over an extended period. This method is particularly effective for drawing out more substantial components like resins, bitter principles, and other water-insoluble compounds.

2.2 The Art of Decoction

To prepare a decoction, start with coarser herbs, such as roots, barks, and seeds. These often possess higher concentrations of active compounds and require prolonged heating to break down their tough cellular structures. By grinding or pounding the plant material before decoction, you can further enhance the extraction process.

Pour about four parts water into a pot for every part of dried plant material. Slowly heat the mixture, bringing it to a gentle simmer. Continue simmering for around 20-30 minutes, or longer for more stubborn plant materials, while occasionally stirring to ensure even heat distribution.

2.3 Benefits and Applications

Decoctions are particularly effective for extracting bitter and astringent constituents, making them well-suited for digestive remedies, tonics, and hair rinses. For instance, a decoction of dandelion root serves as a potent liver tonic, while horsetail decoctions are known to nourish and strengthen hair.

The process of decoction also allows for the extraction of therapeutic minerals and trace elements from the plant material. This makes it an ideal method for obtaining beneficial nutrients such as calcium, potassium, and manganese.

Section 3: Tinctures

3.1 What is a Tincture?

Tinctures are concentrated extracts obtained by soaking plant material in a solvent, usually alcohol, to extract and preserve its active compounds. Alcohol acts as an efficient carrier for both water-soluble and fat-soluble components, making tinctures a highly concentrated and long-lasting herbal remedy.

3.2 The Art of Tincture Making

Tincture making involves selecting the appropriate herb, measuring out the specific parts to be used, and determining the ideal menstruum (liquid used for extraction) and strength. The most common menstruum for tinctures is pure grain alcohol, although other alcohols like vodka or brandy can be used depending on personal preference and the herb being extracted.

To prepare a tincture, chop or grind the plant material to increase its surface area, facilitating better extraction. Add the plant material to a clean glass jar and cover it with the chosen menstruum, ensuring it fully submerges the herbs. Seal the jar and store it in a cool, dark place, shaking the mixture occasionally over several weeks or months to aid extraction.

3.3 Benefits and Applications

Tinctures offer many advantages, including long shelf life, concentrated potency, and easy dosage control. They are widely utilized for their quick and efficient assimilation into the bloodstream, making them suitable for acute health conditions, immune support, and personal care preparations.

Furthermore, tinctures can be combined to create complex herbal formulations and customized blends tailored to suit individual needs. Popular examples include adaptogenic blends for stress management, sleep formulations, and immune-boosting tonics.

In the world of herbal medicine, the art of extraction methods is paramount to unlock the full potential of plants. Infusions, decoctions, and tinctures each possess their unique characteristics, allowing us to harness the vast array of healing compounds nature provides. Experimenting with these techniques opens up a world of possibilities, enabling us to create potent remedies that nourish our bodies and soothe our souls. As we continue our journey, let us explore the intricate and fascinating realm of synergizing plant and human wisdom.

Adapting Techniques for Different Plant Parts

In the world of botany, plants exhibit remarkable diversity in their structure and function. From the towering trees of the rainforest to the delicate flowers in a garden, each plant species has evolved unique adaptations to survive and thrive in their respective environments. One fascinating aspect of plant adaptation is the variety of techniques plants employ to optimize the functioning of different plant parts. In this chapter, we will explore the ingenious strategies that plants have developed to adapt various parts of their anatomy to different functions, including roots, stems, leaves, flowers, and fruits.

1. Adapting Roots:

The root system of a plant serves several critical functions, such as anchoring the plant in the soil, absorbing water and nutrients, and storing reserves. The way plants adapt their roots to perform these functions varies greatly across species. Some plants, like the taproot system found in carrots and dandelions, develop a primary root that grows deep into the soil to access water reserves. Other plants, such as grasses, employ fibrous root systems that spread horizontally near the soil surface, facilitating efficient water absorption.

2. Adapting Stems:

Stems are essential structures that support the plant, transport water and nutrients, and provide areas for photosynthesis. Plants have evolved a myriad of stem adaptations to fulfill these functions. For instance, in climbing plants like ivy, specialized stems called tendrils coil around objects for support, allowing them to reach new heights. Additionally, certain plants, like cacti, developed succulent stems that are capable of storing water in arid environments, ensuring their survival during long periods of drought.

3. Adapting Leaves:

Leaves are perhaps the most recognizable and diverse plant parts. They play a central role in photosynthesis, the process by which plants convert sunlight into energy. To optimize this process, plants have evolved diverse leaf structures, shapes, and sizes. Broad-leafed plants, such as banana trees, possess larger surface areas that capture ample sunlight. Conversely, needle-like leaves found in coniferous trees, like the pine, have reduced surface areas that minimize water loss in dry conditions. Furthermore, some plants exhibit adaptations like thorns, a modified form of leaves, to deter herbivores and minimize water loss.

4. Adapting Flowers:

Flowers are reproductive structures that enable plants to produce seeds, ensuring their survival and reproduction. One remarkable adaptation in flowering plants is the development of colorful petals and fragrances, which attract pollinators such as bees, butterflies, and birds. These adaptations increase the chances of successful pollination and subsequent seed production. Additionally, plants deploy various mechanisms to ensure cross-pollination and prevent self-fertilization, such as producing male and female reproductive parts on separate flowers or releasing pollen at different times.

5. Adapting Fruits:

Fruits are specialized organs that develop from fertilized flowers and serve as a vessel for seed dispersal. The diversity of fruit types is astounding, as plants have adapted their fruits to exploit different methods of dispersal. For instance, fleshy fruits, like apples or berries, are consumed by animals, which subsequently disperse the seeds through their digestive systems. Conversely, plants with dry fruits, such as dandelion or maple trees, produce lightweight seeds that can be dispersed by wind over vast distances.

6. Interactions Among Plant Parts:

While it is essential to understand how plants adapt their individual parts, it is equally important to recognize the complex interactions between these parts. Each plant organ, though specialized, must work in harmony with the others to enable the plant's overall survival and growth. For example, leaves rely on the root system to absorb water, while stems transport nutrients from the roots to the rest of the plant. A disruption in any of these interactions can have adverse effects on the plant's overall health.

Chapter 4: Herbal Pharmacology: Understanding Active Compounds

Herbal medicine has been practiced for centuries and continues to be a significant part of healthcare in many cultures around the world. The healing properties of herbs have been attributed to a vast array of active compounds found within the plant kingdom. In this chapter, we will delve into the fascinating field of herbal pharmacology, exploring the various active compounds present in medicinal plants and their mechanisms of action.

1. Plant Secondary Metabolites:

Plants are complex organisms that produce a wide range of chemical compounds known as secondary metabolites. Unlike primary metabolites that are essential for plant growth and development, secondary metabolites are not directly involved in these processes. Instead, they serve several ecological functions, such as attracting pollinators, defending against pests, and providing protection from environmental stressors.

Many of these secondary metabolites possess medicinal properties and have been harnessed by humans for therapeutic purposes. Some of the key classes of plant secondary metabolites include alkaloids, flavonoids, terpenoids, and phenolic compounds. Within these classes, thousands of different compounds have been identified, each with unique chemical structures and biological activities.

2. Alkaloids:

Alkaloids are a diverse group of nitrogen-containing compounds that exhibit a wide range of pharmacological activities. Some well-known alkaloids include caffeine, morphine, and nicotine. These compounds are commonly found in plants such as the coffee bean, opium poppy, and tobacco leaf, respectively.

The mechanisms of action of alkaloids vary depending on their chemical structure and target receptors or enzymes. For example, morphine exerts its analgesic effect by binding to opioid receptors in the central nervous system, while caffeine acts as a central nervous system stimulant by blocking adenosine receptors.

3. Flavonoids:

Flavonoids are a large class of polyphenolic compounds that are widely distributed in the plant kingdom. They are responsible for the vibrant colors seen in many fruits, vegetables, and flowers. Flavonoids possess diverse biological activities, including antioxidant, anti-inflammatory, and anticancer properties.

The antioxidant activity of flavonoids is crucial for counteracting oxidative stress, which is involved in various diseases, including cardiovascular disease and cancer. Moreover, flavonoids have been shown to modulate enzyme activity and gene expression, leading to their potential therapeutic applications.

4. Terpenoids:

Terpenoids, also known as isoprenoids, are the largest class of plant secondary metabolites. They are responsible for the characteristic scents and flavors of many herbs and spices. Some well-known terpenoids include menthol, found in peppermint, and curcumin, present in turmeric.

Terpenoids exhibit a wide range of pharmacological properties, including antimicrobial, antiviral, and anticancer activities. They can interact with various molecular targets within the body, such as enzymes, receptors, and ion channels. For instance, menthol acts as a topical analgesic by desensitizing sensory nerve endings.

5. Phenolic Compounds:

Phenolic compounds are a diverse group of plant secondary metabolites that are characterized by the presence of a phenol ring. They are found in abundance in many medicinal plants and are known to possess antioxidant, anti-inflammatory, and antimicrobial properties.

One of the most extensively studied phenolic compounds is resveratrol, found in grapes and red wine. Resveratrol has been shown to possess cardio-protective properties, reduce inflammation, and exhibit anticancer effects. Its mechanisms of action involve the modulation of signaling pathways involved in cellular processes such as proliferation, apoptosis, and inflammation.

6. Herbal Drug Interactions:

As herbal medicine gains popularity and becomes integrated with conventional medicine, it is crucial to understand potential interactions between herbal drugs and conventional pharmaceuticals. Active compounds in herbs can modulate the activity of drug-metabolizing enzymes, transporters, and receptors, which can affect the pharmacokinetics and pharmacodynamics of co-administered drugs.

For example, St. John's Wort, a popular herbal remedy for depression, induces the expression of drug-metabolizing enzymes in the liver, leading to decreased plasma concentrations of various medications, including oral contraceptives and antiretroviral drugs. Such interactions can result in decreased efficacy or increased toxicity of the co-administered drugs.

Chapter 4 explored the fascinating world of herbal pharmacology, focusing on the various active compounds present in medicinal plants. We learned about alkaloids, flavonoids, terpenoids, and phenolic compounds, and their diverse pharmacological properties. Understanding these active compounds and their mechanisms of action is crucial in harnessing the therapeutic potential of herbal medicine while ensuring safe and effective use in combination with conventional pharmaceuticals.

The Chemical Complexity of Plants

Plants, with their vibrant colors, graceful shapes, and seductive fragrances, have been a subject of fascination for humans throughout history. While their aesthetic appeal is undeniable, it is their chemical complexity that truly captivates us and unlocks their remarkable potential. From the delicate petals of a rose to the towering branches of a redwood tree, plants possess an incredible array of chemical compounds that govern their growth, development, and interactions with other organisms. In this chapter, we will delve into the fascinating world of plant chemistry, exploring the diverse compounds and their functions that make plants such an intriguing and essential part of our natural world.

The Building Blocks: Primary Metabolites

Every living organism requires a set of fundamental compounds to carry out its basic physiological functions, and plants are no exception. These primary metabolites serve as the building blocks for the synthesis of more complex compounds and are involved in essential processes such as photosynthesis, respiration, and growth.

One of the critical primary metabolites found in plants is glucose, a simple sugar and the primary source of energy. Glucose is produced during photosynthesis, where plants convert sunlight, water, and carbon dioxide into chemical energy. Furthermore, glucose serves as a precursor for the synthesis of other essential molecules like cellulose, a structural component of plant cell walls, and starch, which serves as a long-term energy storage.

Another primary metabolite, amino acids, plays a central role in plant biochemistry. Amino acids form the building blocks of proteins, which are vital for plant growth and development. Additionally, some amino acids function as signaling molecules and serve as precursors for the synthesis of hormones, defense compounds, and secondary metabolites.

Secondary Metabolites: The Chemical Arsenal

Beyond their primary metabolites, plants possess an astonishing variety of secondary metabolites, which are compounds not directly involved in basic physiological functions but play crucial roles in the plant's interaction with its environment. These compounds contribute to plant defense against pathogens, herbivores, and adverse environmental conditions.

Among the secondary metabolites, alkaloids stand out as one of the most diverse and chemically fascinating groups. These nitrogen-containing compounds are found in plants across various families and exhibit an array of biological activities. Alkaloids can act as potent toxins, repellents, or attractants, making them crucial for plant defense and communication. Well-known examples include caffeine, nicotine, and morphine, each with its distinct effects on humans and animals.

Terpenoids, another prominent group of secondary metabolites, are responsible for the captivating aromas associated with many plants. These compounds are derived from a common building block called isoprene and encompass a wide range of structures and functions. Terpenoids play vital roles in attracting pollinators, deterring herbivores, and protecting plants from microbial infections.

Phenolic compounds, such as flavonoids and tannins, are yet another class of secondary metabolites found abundantly in plants. These compounds provide pigmentation to flowers, fruits, and leaves, contributing to the visual appeal of plants. Additionally, phenolics play significant roles as antioxidants, protecting plants from oxidative stress and ultraviolet radiation. Furthermore, they can have antimicrobial and anti-inflammatory properties, making them valuable for human health as well.

The Hidden Network: Plant Hormones

In addition to their primary and secondary metabolites, plants rely on a complex network of signaling molecules called plant hormones or phytohormones to regulate various aspects of their growth and development. These hormones orchestrate processes such as seed germination, root and shoot growth, flowering, fruit ripening, and senescence.

Auxins, the first group of plant hormones to be discovered, play a crucial role in plant growth and development. They are involved in promoting cell elongation, tropisms, and the formation of adventitious roots. Additionally, auxins regulate apical dominance, controlling the growth and development of lateral buds.

Gibberellins, another important group of hormones, primarily influence stem elongation and seed germination. These hormones stimulate cell division, elongation, and differentiation, allowing plants to exhibit rapid growth responses under favorable conditions. Cytokinins, as their name suggests, promote cell division and affect various aspects of plant growth and development. They are involved in regulating shoot and root development, leaf senescence, and bud activation.

Ethylene, a gaseous hormone, plays a crucial role in plant responses to mechanical stress, senescence, and fruit ripening. Although it is one of the simplest plant hormones, ethylene exerts a broad range of effects on plant physiology and development.

Interactions with the Environment: Chemical Ecology

Plants do not exist in isolation; they constantly interact with other organisms, including herbivores, pathogens, and symbiotic partners. The chemical compounds produced by plants play a vital role in mediating these interactions, shaping the delicate balance between survival and reproduction.

One remarkable example of plant chemical ecology is the phenomenon of allelopathy. Some plants release allelochemicals, secondary metabolites that inhibit the germination or growth of other plants in their vicinity. These chemicals give the releasing plant a competitive advantage by reducing resource availability or deterring potential herbivores.

Plant-pathogen interactions also heavily rely on chemical communication. Plants produce an array of compounds, such as phytoalexins and volatile organic compounds, to defend against invading pathogens. Conversely, pathogens can secrete enzymes and toxins that manipulate plant metabolism and evade plant defense mechanisms.

Furthermore, plants forge intricate relationships with beneficial microorganisms, such as mycorrhizal fungi and nitrogen-fixing bacteria, through chemical signaling. Plants release specific compounds that attract these beneficial organisms, which, in turn, provide nutrients or protection against pathogens.

The chemical complexity of plants is an awe-inspiring characteristic that underlies their survival and prosperity. From the primary metabolites that sustain basic functions to the secondary metabolites that contribute to the plant's defense and ecological interactions, plants have evolved an astonishing assortment of chemical compounds. Understanding these chemicals and their functions not only enriches our knowledge of the natural world but also holds promise for applications in various fields, including medicine, agriculture, and industry. By unraveling the intricate web of plant chemistry, we can unlock the untapped potential of these remarkable organisms and foster a greater appreciation for their essential role in the biological tapestry of life.

Key Phytochemicals and Their Effects

In recent years, there has been a growing interest in the role of phytochemicals in promoting human health. These natural substances are found abundantly in plants and have been extensively studied for their potential health benefits. Phytochemicals are known to possess various biological activities that may contribute to the prevention and treatment of chronic diseases, including cancer, cardiovascular diseases, and neurodegenerative disorders.

This chapter aims to explore some of the key phytochemicals that have gained significant attention in scientific research and their potential effects on human health. We will delve into the chemical structures, dietary sources, and mechanisms of action underlying the health-promoting properties of these fascinating compounds.

1. Resveratrol:

Resveratrol, a naturally occurring polyphenol, has gained tremendous attention due to its potential health benefits. It is primarily found in grapes, berries, and some nuts. Resveratrol exhibits antioxidant, anti-inflammatory, and anti-carcinogenic properties, making it a promising candidate for the prevention and treatment of various diseases.

Studies have shown that resveratrol exerts cardioprotective effects by reducing oxidative stress, inhibiting inflammation, and improving lipid profile and blood pressure. Additionally, it has been found to modulate signaling pathways involved in cancer development, suppressing the growth of tumor cells and inducing apoptosis. Moreover, resveratrol has been associated with neuroprotective effects, potentially reducing the risk of neurodegenerative disorders such as Alzheimer's and Parkinson's diseases.

2. Curcumin:

Curcumin, the active component of turmeric, has been used for centuries in traditional medicine due to its medicinal properties. It exhibits potent antioxidant and anti-inflammatory effects, making it an interesting subject of research in various human health conditions.

Curcumin has been extensively studied for its potential roles in cancer prevention and treatment. It has demonstrated anti-proliferative and anti-metastatic effects in various types of cancer, including breast, colon, and pancreatic cancers. Furthermore, curcumin's ability to modulate multiple signaling pathways involved in inflammation has shown promise in managing chronic inflammatory diseases such as rheumatoid arthritis.

Another intriguing aspect of curcumin is its neuroprotective potential. It has been suggested to enhance cognitive functions and delay the progression of neurodegenerative disorders by reducing oxidative stress, inflammation, and amyloid-beta plaque accumulation in the brain.

3. Quercetin:

Quercetin is a flavonoid widely distributed in fruits, vegetables, and grains. It possesses antioxidant, anti-inflammatory, and anti-carcinogenic properties. Research suggests that quercetin may contribute to human health by preventing chronic diseases and promoting overall well-being.

Antioxidant properties of quercetin enable it to scavenge free radicals and reduce oxidative stress, thereby protecting cells from damage and reducing the risk of chronic diseases such as cancer and cardiovascular diseases. Additionally, quercetin has been shown to inhibit the growth of cancer cells, induce apoptosis, and interfere with angiogenesis, the process of forming blood vessels that supply tumors.

Furthermore, quercetin's potential benefits extend to cardiovascular health as it exhibits anti-hypertensive and anti-atherosclerotic effects. It also possesses anti-allergic and anti-inflammatory properties, which may contribute to managing allergic disorders, asthma, and other inflammatory conditions.

4. Epigallocatechin gallate (EGCG):

EGCG, a catechin present in high concentrations in green tea, has gained considerable attention for its wide range of health benefits. It exhibits antioxidant, anti-inflammatory, and anti-cancer properties, making it a subject of significant interest in scientific research.

EGCG has been shown to have chemopreventive effects by inhibiting the growth and proliferation of cancer cells, inducing apoptosis, and inhibiting angiogenesis and metastasis. It has demonstrated promising results in various cancers, including breast, prostate, and lung cancers.

Furthermore, EGCG's antioxidant activity contributes to its cardioprotective effects by reducing oxidative stress and inflammation, preventing the progression of atherosclerosis, and improving lipid profile. It has also been associated with neuroprotective effects, potentially reducing the risk of neurodegenerative diseases by modulating signaling pathways involved in neuronal survival and cognitive functions.

Synergy and the Entourage Effect

In the magnificent tapestry of nature, various plant compounds have evolved to work harmoniously, creating potent and diverse effects. Humans have long harnessed the power of these botanical wonders, crafting remedies that have stood the test of time. While scientific research has advanced our understanding, a fascinating phenomenon known as synergy and the entourage effect continue to captivate researchers and enthusiasts alike. This chapter explores the intricacies and significance of these phenomena, shedding light on how the whole often surpasses the sum of its parts.

The Entourage Effect: An Orchestra of Plant-Driven Harmony

When examining the therapeutic potential of plant compounds, many scientists and researchers have shifted their focus from isolating individual components to examining the collective influence of multiple compounds in a plant. Termed the "entourage effect," this phenomenon suggests that the combined action of various compounds produces superior therapeutic effects compared to isolated components.

For instance, let us consider the cannabis plant. The two most well-known compounds within cannabis are tetrahydrocannabinol (THC) and cannabidiol (CBD). Researchers have discovered that when consumed together, these two compounds interact synergistically to modulate the psychoactive effects of THC and provide additional therapeutic benefits. The unremitting cooperation of the diverse compounds in the plant kingdom forms the basis of the entourage effect, affording us a deeper insight into the intricacies of nature's pharmacopeia.

Synergy: The Power of Collaboration

Synergy, a concept rooted in the Greek word "synergos" meaning "working together," highlights the majestic ways in which nature's botanical compounds synergistically unite to unleash profound biological effects. Just as a symphony of instruments creates a more remarkable melody than any single instrument played alone, the symphony of plant compounds engages in a sophisticated interplay to amplify therapeutic properties.

A prominent example of synergistic power can be observed in essential oils. These complex aromatic compounds, extracted and distilled from various plants, are known to possess unique healing properties. However, it is when these compounds interact synergistically that their true potential unfolds.

Consider the refreshing aroma of a lavender field. Lavender oil, one of the most extensively studied essential oils, comprises several bioactive compounds, such as linalool, linalyl acetate, and terpinen-4-ol. When these compounds converge, their combined effect surpasses the individual actions, resulting in a deeply calming and stress-relieving experience. Synergy allows for the harmonization of different properties, transforming a blend of compounds into a potent force for holistic healing.

Exploring the Complexity of Entourage Effect

While the entourage effect is most often associated with cannabis, its underlying mechanisms extend far beyond this remarkable plant. The entourage effect can manifest in various botanical compositions, revealing the extent of nature's complexity.

One such example lies within the tea plant, Camellia sinensis. Although tea is commonly enjoyed for its caffeine content, it also possesses an array of phytochemical compounds, including catechins, theanine, and flavonoids. The complex interplay between these constituents impacts the flavor, aroma, and overall experiential value of tea. Each compound brings its unique contribution, resulting in delicate variations and nuances to this beloved beverage. Much like a piece of music performed by an ensemble, the entourage effect in tea creates a sensory symphony that transcends the sum of its parts.

Additionally, the entourage effect can be found in the realm of herbal medicine. Take, for instance, the traditional Ayurvedic formulation of Triphala. Consisting of three fruit powders, Amla (Emblica officinalis), Haritaki (Terminalia chebula), and Bibhitaki (Terminalia bellirica), Triphala embodies the principles of synergy. These fruits, when combined, work in harmony to enhance digestion, promote detoxification, and offer a myriad of other health benefits. Similar to a skilled trio of musicians, each fruit contributes its strengths, resulting in a harmonious composition of healing properties.

Beyond Plant Compounds: The Role of Supporting Agents

While the entourage effect primarily emphasizes the collaboration of various plant compounds, it is crucial not to overlook the supporting characters in this botanical symphony. Co-factors, often referred to as "accessory compounds," play an essential role in regulating and enhancing the effects of the primary compounds.

In the world of herbal medicine, these co-factors can include enzymes, antioxidants, carrier molecules, and even minerals. These compounds often work in tandem to promote greater bioavailability, catalyze reactions or enable compounds to reach their intended target effectively. By harmonizing and optimizing a plant's therapeutic potential, these accessory compounds become integral to achieving the full synergistic experience offered by nature.

Unlocking Nature's Secrets: Unraveling the Complexity

Despite the remarkable progress made in understanding synergy and the entourage effect, numerous questions remain unanswered. The complexities of plant chemistry and the interplay of various constituents continually challenge researchers to explore further and uncover nature's secrets.

Rigorous scientific inquiry with comprehensive analytical techniques has shown promise in unveiling the mysteries behind synergy in plants. Scientists employ methods such as metabolomics, transcriptomics, and proteomics to decode the intricate webs of interactions within plants. These approaches enable the identification and characterization of previously unknown bioactive compounds, providing valuable insights into the mechanisms driving synergy.

In As we traverse the botanical landscape, we come face-to-face with the remarkable phenomena of synergy and the entourage effect. By understanding and celebrating the harmonious relationships between plant compounds and their supporting agents, we can unlock the full potential of nature's botanical symphony.

Acknowledging the captivating properties unveiled through the entourage effect and harnessing the power of synergy, we can embark on novel avenues of research. By expanding our knowledge and appreciation of these magical interactions, we inch closer to uncovering the profound secrets hidden within the botanical world, forever inspiring awe and driving innovation.

Chapter 5: Herbs for Digestive Health

In today's fast-paced world, maintaining digestive health has become increasingly challenging. With poor dietary choices, high stress levels, and sedentary lifestyles, it's no wonder that many individuals experience digestive issues. From bloating and indigestion to irritable bowel syndrome (IBS) and gastritis, these ailments can significantly impact one's quality of life. Thankfully, nature provides us with a wide array of herbs that can promote digestive health and restore balance to our gut. In this chapter, we will explore some of the most effective herbs for digestive health, their benefits, and how to incorporate them into our daily lives.

1. Peppermint (Mentha piperita):

Peppermint is a renowned herb known for its ability to soothe various digestive ailments. Its main active component, menthol, possesses antispasmodic properties that help calm the muscles of the gastrointestinal tract. This makes it particularly useful for relieving symptoms of bloating, flatulence, and cramping. Peppermint can also promote healthy digestion by stimulating the production of digestive enzymes, allowing for better breakdown and absorption of nutrients.

To enjoy the benefits of peppermint, try sipping on a cup of peppermint tea after a meal or taking enteric-coated peppermint oil capsules. However, it is important to note that peppermint may worsen symptoms in individuals with gastroesophageal reflux disease (GERD) or hiatal hernias.

2. Chamomile (Matricaria chamomilla):

Chamomile has been used for centuries due to its calming and anti-inflammatory properties. This herb not only aids in digestion but also helps alleviate stress and anxiety, which can contribute to digestive disturbances. Chamomile tea is a popular choice for relieving indigestion, gastritis, and stomach cramps.

To prepare chamomile tea, steep dried Chamomile flowers in hot water for 5-10 minutes, then strain and drink. Adding a bit of honey or lemon can enhance the flavor and provide extra benefits. It is important to ensure that you are not allergic to chamomile before consuming it regularly.

3. Ginger (Zingiber officinale):

Ginger is a potent herb well-known for its digestive benefits. Its active compounds, gingerols, promote healthy digestion by increasing the production of digestive enzymes, reducing inflammation, and accelerating gastric emptying. Ginger has been extensively studied for its efficacy in reducing nausea, vomiting, and other symptoms associated with motion sickness, morning sickness, and chemotherapy-induced nausea.

To incorporate ginger into your routine, you can add fresh grated ginger to your meals, brew ginger tea, or take ginger capsules.

However, individuals with gallstones or on blood-thinning medications should consult their healthcare provider before consuming ginger in large amounts.

4. Fennel (Foeniculum vulgare):

Fennel is an aromatic herb with a distinct licorice-like flavor. It has long been used as a natural remedy to aid digestion and relieve symptoms of gastrointestinal discomfort. Fennel seeds contain various essential oils and volatile compounds that possess anti-inflammatory and antispasmodic properties. These properties make fennel an excellent choice for alleviating bloating, colic, and indigestion.

To reap the benefits of fennel, chew on fennel seeds after meals or drink fennel tea. Fennel tea can be prepared by steeping crushed fennel seeds in hot water for 10-15 minutes. It is important to note that fennel may interact with certain medications, including blood thinners and estrogen-based contraceptives.

5. Slippery Elm (Ulmus rubra):

Slippery Elm is a herb derived from the inner bark of the Slippery Elm tree. It has a long history of use in traditional medicine for its soothing and protective effects on the digestive tract. The mucilage content in Slippery Elm creates a gel-like substance that coats the stomach and intestines, reducing inflammation and protecting the lining from irritants.

Slippery Elm is available in various forms, including capsules, lozenges, and powders. Mixing the powder with water creates a soothing drink that can relieve heartburn, gastritis, and symptoms of inflammatory bowel disease (IBD). It is advisable to take Slippery Elm separately from medications, as it may interfere with their absorption.

In this chapter, we have delved into the therapeutic properties of some of nature's most beneficial herbs for digestive health. Peppermint, chamomile, ginger, fennel, and slippery elm all offer unique benefits that can alleviate common digestive complaints and promote overall gut health. Remember that while herbs can be powerful allies on the path to wellness, it's always essential to consult with a healthcare professional before incorporating them into your routine, especially if you have underlying health conditions or are taking medications. By embracing these herbs and incorporating them into a balanced lifestyle, you can take charge of your digestive health and experience improved overall well-being.

Soothing Upset Stomachs and Indigestion

We've all experienced the discomfort of an upset stomach at some point in our lives. Whether it's due to overindulgence, stress, or certain types of food, indigestion can be a real nuisance. The good news is that there are several natural remedies and techniques that can help soothe your upset stomach and alleviate indigestion. In this chapter, we will explore some of these tried-and-true methods, enabling you to find relief and get back to feeling your best. So, grab a cup of herbal tea, get comfortable, and let's delve into the world of soothing upset stomachs and indigestion.

Understanding Upset Stomachs and Indigestion

Before we can find effective remedies, it's important to have a basic understanding of what causes upset stomachs and indigestion. Indigestion, also known as dyspepsia, occurs when there's a disruption in the digestive process. This disruption can result in a range of uncomfortable symptoms, including abdominal pain, bloating, heartburn, nausea, and gas.

There are various factors that contribute to indigestion, such as eating too quickly, overeating, consuming high-fat or spicy foods, and even the presence of certain medical conditions like gastroesophageal reflux disease (GERD). Stress and anxiety can also lead to an upset stomach, as they can disrupt the normal functioning of the digestive system.

Now that we have a better understanding of what causes an upset stomach, let's explore some natural remedies that can bring relief.

1. Ginger: The Digestive Superstar

Ginger has been used for centuries to soothe upset stomachs and aid digestion. Its active compounds, gingerols and shogaols, have powerful anti-inflammatory and antioxidant properties that can alleviate nausea and reduce the severity of indigestion symptoms. To reap the benefits of ginger, you can either chew on a small piece of fresh ginger, sip on ginger tea, or take ginger supplements.

2. Peppermint: Cooling Comfort for Your Stomach

Peppermint has long been recognized for its ability to calm an upset stomach. It contains menthol, a compound that helps relax the muscles of the gastrointestinal tract, allowing for smoother digestion. Peppermint can be consumed in various forms, including peppermint tea, capsules, or diluted essential oil. However, it's essential to note that peppermint oil should be used with caution, as it can worsen symptoms in people with gastroesophageal reflux disease (GERD).

3. Chamomile: A Soothing Herbal Elixir

Chamomile tea is not only a delightful beverage but also an excellent remedy for indigestion. It possesses anti-inflammatory properties that can relieve abdominal pain and soothe irritated stomachs. Additionally, chamomile has muscle-relaxing effects, promoting smoother digestion and reducing bloating. Sipping on a warm cup of chamomile tea after a meal can work wonders for calming your stomach.

4. Probiotics: Nurturing Your Gut Health

Maintaining a healthy balance of gut bacteria is crucial for optimal digestion. Probiotics are live bacteria and yeasts that can aid in the breakdown and absorption of food, preventing indigestion. They can be found in certain fermented foods like yogurt, kefir, sauerkraut, and kimchi. Alternatively, probiotic supplements are widely available and can help replenish the natural bacteria in your gut.

5. Mindful Eating: Savoring Every Bite

In today's fast-paced world, we often overlook the importance of mindful eating. Eating quickly and mindlessly can lead to overeating and indigestion. To prevent this, take the time to fully savor each bite, chew your food thoroughly, and pause between mouthfuls. Additionally, try to eat in a calm and relaxed environment, away from distractions. By practicing mindful eating, you give your body the time it needs to digest properly, reducing the risk of an upset stomach.

6. Herbal Remedies: Nature's Digestive Support

Nature provides us with a wide array of plants and herbs that can aid digestion and soothe upset stomachs. For example, fennel seeds have been used for centuries as a digestive aid, helping to alleviate bloating and stomach cramps. Similarly, dandelion root has a long history of traditional use in supporting healthy digestion. These herbal remedies can be prepared as teas, tinctures, or capsules, providing a gentle and natural way to ease indigestion.

7. Aromatherapy: Fragrant Relief

Aromatherapy is a complementary therapy that utilizes the aromatic properties of essential oils to promote healing and relaxation. When it comes to upset stomachs and indigestion, certain essential oils can be highly beneficial. For instance, lavender oil is known for its calming effects and can help reduce stress-related digestive issues. On the other hand, lemon essential oil has been used to stimulate digestion and alleviate symptoms of indigestion. Dilute a few drops of your favorite essential oil in a carrier oil and gently massage onto your abdomen for a soothing experience.

Soothing upset stomachs and indigestion doesn't need to involve reaching for over-the-counter medications. By incorporating natural remedies and adopting healthy habits, we can alleviate discomfort and promote better digestion. From ginger to chamomile tea, probiotics to mindful eating, Nature has blessed us with a plethora of tools to support our digestive health. So, the next time your stomach feels uneasy, remember the wisdom of these natural remedies and take the necessary steps towards finding relief.

Bitters and Their Role in Digestion

When it comes to digestion, we often think about the important role played by stomach acid and various enzymes. However, there is another key component that is frequently overlooked – the use of bitters. Bitters have been used for centuries across different cultures as a natural remedy to improve digestion and enhance overall health. In this chapter, we will delve into the fascinating world of bitters, exploring their origins, their impact on digestion, and their potential health benefits. Join us as we uncover the hidden secrets behind these powerful botanical allies and discover the wonders they hold for our well-being.

Section 1: The Origins of Bitters

1.1 Ancient Roots:

The use of bitter herbs and plants for medicinal purposes dates back to ancient times. Ancient Egyptians, Greeks, and Romans recognized the digestive benefits of consuming bitters and regularly ingested them to aid digestion and promote overall health. The works of prominent physicians such as Hippocrates and Galen emphasized the significance of bitters in maintaining a balanced digestive system. Even today, traditional medicine systems like Ayurveda and Traditional Chinese Medicine continue to utilize bitters to support digestion and promote well-being.

1.2 Evolution of Bitters:

Through the ages, the practice of using bitters has evolved, with different cultures and regions incorporating their unique botanicals into the mix. In Europe, iconic bitters such as Swedish Bitters and Italian Amari gained popularity, showcasing the cultural diversity and rich traditions surrounding bitters. New World explorers also discovered various bitter plants, such as dandelion and gentian, which indigenous populations had long used for medicinal purposes. These discoveries led to the development of a wide range of bitters that are still popular today.

Section 2: Understanding Bitters

2.1 Composition of Bitters:

Bitters are typically made from a combination of bitter botanicals, which may include roots, leaves, barks, fruits, and flowers. These botanicals contain compounds known as bitter principles, such as alkaloids and glycosides, which provide the characteristic bitter taste. Some common bitter botanicals found in many bitters blends include gentian, wormwood, dandelion, artichoke, and burdock. Additionally, bitters may often be infused with other herbs and spices to add complexity and flavor to the mixture.

2.2 How Bitters Work:

When consumed, bitters stimulate the taste receptors on our tongue, triggering a cascade of reactions in the body. The bitter taste receptors are connected to our digestive system, signaling the secretion of digestive juices, such as gastric acid, saliva, and bile. This enhanced secretion improves the breakdown and absorption of nutrients, making it easier for our bodies to extract essential vitamins and minerals from the food we consume. Bitters also help relax smooth muscle in the digestive tract, aiding in proper gastrointestinal motility and reducing symptoms such as bloating and constipation.

2.3 Classification of Bitters:

Bitters can be classified into three main categories based on their primary action: hepatic, digestive, and appetizing bitters.

2.3.1 Hepatic Bitters:

Hepatic bitters primarily target the liver, aiding in detoxification and maintaining the overall health of this vital organ. They stimulate the liver to produce and secrete bile, which plays a crucial role in the digestion and absorption of fats. Popular hepatic bitter herbs include milk thistle, dandelion root, and burdock root.

2.3.2 Digestive Bitters:

Digestive bitters focus on enhancing digestion by stimulating the secretion of digestive juices and enzymes. They can help alleviate indigestion, flatulence, and acid reflux by promoting optimal stomach acid production and supporting the activity of pancreatic enzymes. Some notable digestive bitter herbs include gentian, wormwood, chamomile, and ginger.

2.3.3 Appetizing Bitters:

Appetizing bitters are ideal for individuals who struggle with poor appetite or sluggish digestion. These bitters stimulate not only the liver and digestion but also the taste buds, helping to increase appetite and improve the overall digestive experience. Common appetizing bitter herbs include blessed thistle, angelica, and orange peel.

Section 3: The Health Benefits of Bitters

3.1 Digestive Health:

One of the primary benefits of incorporating bitters into our daily routine is improved digestive health. By stimulating the digestive juices and enhancing the breakdown and absorption of nutrients, bitters can help combat digestive issues such as bloating, gas, and indigestion. Regular consumption of bitters may also contribute to an overall healthy gut microbiome, supporting the growth of beneficial bacteria.

3.2 Liver Support:

The liver plays a crucial role in detoxification and maintaining our overall well-being. Bitters that target hepatic function can support the liver's detoxification processes, potentially aiding in the elimination of toxins from the body. Additionally, by stimulating bile production, hepatic bitters can improve fat digestion and absorption.

3.3 Improved Nutrient Absorption:

The enhanced secretion of digestive juices and enzymes triggered by bitters leads to improved breakdown and absorption of nutrients from the food we eat. This can have a positive impact on our nutrient status, supporting overall well-being and preventing nutrient deficiencies.

3.4 Appetite Stimulation:

Many individuals struggle with a poor appetite, leading to inadequate intake of essential nutrients. Appetizing bitters can help address this issue by stimulating the taste buds and enhancing the desire to eat. By kickstarting the digestive process, these bitters can support increased appetite and improve overall nutritional intake.

Section 4: Incorporating Bitters into Daily Life

4.1 Choosing the Right Bitters:

With the wide variety of bitters available, it is essential to select the one that suits your specific needs and preferences. Consider factors such as the herbs used, the intended primary action (hepatic, digestive, or appetizing), and the desired flavor profile when making your selection. It may be helpful to consult with a healthcare professional or herbalist to determine the most suitable bitters for your unique digestive concerns.

4.2 Dosage and Consumption:

Bitters can be consumed in various forms, including tinctures, herbal teas, or even added directly to meals and beverages. When using bitters, it is essential to follow the recommended dosage instructions provided by the manufacturer or an herbal practitioner. Start with a low dosage initially, gradually increasing as needed. It is always recommended to consult with a healthcare professional before incorporating bitters into your routine, particularly if you are pregnant, breastfeeding, or have any underlying health conditions. In this chapter, we have explored the fascinating world of bitters and their crucial role in digestion. From their ancient roots to their modern-day usage, bitters have proven to be valuable allies in maintaining optimal digestive health. By embracing these bitter botanicals and their many health benefits, we can unlock a world of improved digestion, enhanced nutrient absorption, and overall well-being. Remember to consult with a healthcare professional before starting any new herbal regimen, and enjoy the journey of discovering the wonders of bitters for yourself.

Managing Gastrointestinal Disorders Naturally

The gastrointestinal system plays a crucial role in our overall health and well-being. It is responsible for the digestion and absorption of nutrients, the elimination of waste, and the maintenance of a strong immune system. However, millions of people around the world suffer from various gastrointestinal disorders, such as irritable bowel syndrome (IBS), acid reflux, gastritis, and inflammatory bowel disease (IBD). While conventional medications can offer relief, they often come with adverse side effects. Therefore, many individuals are turning to natural remedies to manage their gastrointestinal disorders safely and effectively. In this chapter, we will explore some of the natural approaches that can bring relief and promote optimal gastrointestinal health.

Dietary Modifications

One of the first steps in managing gastrointestinal disorders naturally is to make dietary modifications. Certain foods can trigger symptoms and exacerbate existing conditions. For instance, individuals with IBS often find that high-fiber foods, fatty foods, caffeine, alcohol, and spicy foods can worsen their symptoms. By identifying and eliminating trigger foods, individuals can experience significant relief. It is recommended to keep a food diary to track symptoms and identify specific foods that may be causing distress.

Additionally, incorporating foods that are gentle on the digestive system, such as cooked vegetables, lean proteins, whole grains, and fermented foods, can promote healing and soothe gastrointestinal inflammation.

Probiotics

The use of probiotics has gained immense popularity in recent years, with numerous studies highlighting their positive effects on gastrointestinal health. Probiotics are live bacteria and yeasts that provide a range of health benefits when consumed. They work by replenishing and restoring the natural balance of gut bacteria, which can become disrupted in gastrointestinal disorders. Research has shown that probiotics can alleviate symptoms of IBS, reduce inflammation in the gut, and improve overall digestive function. These beneficial microorganisms can be found in various fermented foods, such as yogurt, sauerkraut, kimchi, and kefir. Alternatively, probiotic supplements are widely available and offer a convenient way to ensure an adequate intake of these beneficial bacteria.

Herbal Remedies

Herbal remedies have been used for centuries to relieve gastrointestinal symptoms and promote digestive health. Here are some popular herbs that have shown promising results in managing gastrointestinal disorders naturally:

1. Peppermint: Peppermint has been a go-to remedy for digestive

issues due to its soothing properties. It helps to relax the muscles of the gastrointestinal tract, which can reduce abdominal pain, bloating, and gas. Peppermint tea or peppermint oil capsules can be taken to alleviate symptoms.

2. Ginger: Ginger is widely known for its anti-inflammatory and anti-nausea properties. Its ability to reduce inflammation in the gastrointestinal tract makes it an excellent choice for managing conditions such as gastritis and IBD. Adding fresh ginger to meals, drinking ginger tea, or taking ginger supplements can provide relief.

3. Chamomile: Chamomile is a gentle herb that can calm the digestive system and relieve symptoms of indigestion, acid reflux, and IBS. It has anti-inflammatory properties and can also help relax the muscles of the gastrointestinal tract. Chamomile tea is a popular and effective remedy for gastrointestinal discomfort.

Stress Management

Stress is closely linked to gastrointestinal disorders, as it can exacerbate symptoms and impact the overall health of the digestive system. Therefore, incorporating stress management techniques is vital for managing these conditions naturally. Regular exercise, meditation, deep breathing exercises, and yoga can all help reduce stress and promote relaxation. Finding time for activities that bring joy and relaxation, such as hobbies or spending time in nature, is equally important. Additionally, seeking professional help from therapists or counselors can provide additional support in managing stress and its impact on overall health.

Lifestyle Modifications

In addition to dietary changes, herbal remedies, and stress management, making certain lifestyle modifications can significantly improve gastrointestinal health. Here are a few essential tips to consider:

1. Stay hydrated: Drinking adequate amounts of water throughout the day is crucial for maintaining optimal digestive function. Water helps soften stool and prevents constipation, a common symptom in gastrointestinal disorders.

2. Chew food thoroughly: Properly chewing food aids in digestion by breaking down food into smaller particles. This ensures that the gastrointestinal system can digest and absorb nutrients effectively.

3. Avoid overeating: Consuming large meals can put additional strain on the digestive system, leading to discomfort and exacerbation of symptoms. Opting for smaller, more frequent meals can promote digestion and reduce symptoms.

4. Quit smoking and limit alcohol intake: Smoking and excessive alcohol consumption can irritate the gastrointestinal tract, leading to inflammation and exacerbating symptoms of various disorders. Quitting smoking and moderating alcohol intake can have significant benefits for overall gastrointestinal health.

Managing gastrointestinal disorders naturally requires a comprehensive approach that includes dietary modifications, probiotics, herbal remedies, stress management, and lifestyle modifications. By addressing the root cause of the symptoms and promoting optimal digestive health, individuals can achieve long-lasting relief and improve their quality of life. It is important to note that while these natural approaches can offer significant benefits, it is always advisable to consult a healthcare professional before making any changes, especially if you have a pre-existing medical condition or are currently on medication.

Modern Research on Digestive-Boosting Herbs

Throughout history, humans have relied on plants to nourish and heal their bodies. Traditional herbal medicine systems around the world have long recognized the importance of digestive health in maintaining overall well-being. Today, in the age of scientific advancements, researchers continue to explore the potential of various herbs to support digestive function. This chapter delves into modern research on digestive-boosting herbs, uncovering their active compounds, mechanisms of action, and evidence-backed benefits.

Understanding Digestive Health

The digestive system plays a vital role in breaking down food, absorbing nutrients, and eliminating waste from the body. However, factors such as a poor diet, stress, and sedentary lifestyle can disrupt this delicate balance, leading to discomfort and health issues ranging from heartburn and bloating to more serious conditions like irritable bowel syndrome (IBS) and inflammatory bowel disease (IBD).

To enhance digestive health, herbal remedies have gained popularity due to their potential therapeutic properties. These herbs not only possess active compounds that promote digestion but also exhibit anti-inflammatory, anti-microbial, and antioxidant effects, which can alleviate many digestive ailments and support the growth of beneficial gut bacteria.

Peppermint: A Soothing Ally

Peppermint (Mentha x piperita), a hybrid of watermint and spearmint, is widely known for its refreshing aroma and flavor. Traditional medicine has revered peppermint for its carminative properties, helping to relieve gastrointestinal discomfort and spasms. Modern research has elucidated the mechanisms behind its digestive benefits and identified key active compounds responsible for its effects.

Menthol, the primary active compound in peppermint, acts as a smooth muscle relaxant, reducing spasms in the digestive tract. This herb has shown promise in treating symptoms of IBS, such as abdominal pain and bloating. A randomized controlled trial involving IBS patients observed that peppermint oil capsules significantly reduced their symptoms compared to a placebo group.

Moreover, peppermint can also alleviate symptoms associated with gastroesophageal reflux disease (GERD), attributed to its ability to relax the lower esophageal sphincter and prevent acid reflux. Research suggests that consumption of peppermint tea or supplementation with enteric-coated peppermint oil capsules can provide relief from heartburn and improve overall digestive health.

Ginger: A Time-Honored Wonder

Ginger (Zingiber officinale), a culinary spice and medicinal herb, has long been revered for its digestive properties in traditional medicine systems such as Ayurveda and Traditional Chinese Medicine (TCM). This multitasking herb stimulates digestion, reduces inflammation, and aids in the absorption of nutrients.

The active compounds in ginger, gingerol, and shogaol, are responsible for its myriad health benefits, particularly its digestive effects. Ginger stimulates the secretion of digestive enzymes, improves gut motility, and relieves nausea and vomiting.

Clinical trials have demonstrated ginger's efficacy in managing various digestive disorders. In a study involving pregnant women experiencing nausea and vomiting, ginger supplementation significantly reduced symptoms. Additionally, ginger has shown promise in alleviating symptoms associated with dyspepsia, a condition characterized by chronic indigestion and discomfort.

Turmeric: A Spice for Digestive Harmony

Turmeric (Curcuma longa), a vibrant yellow spice widely used in Indian cuisine, has gained considerable attention for its potent anti-inflammatory properties. Curcumin, the primary active compound in turmeric, is responsible for these effects and has been extensively studied for its therapeutic benefits in digestive health.
Studies have shown that curcumin can help protect the gastrointestinal lining by reducing inflammation caused by

conditions such as ulcerative colitis and Crohn's disease. Curcumin's antioxidant properties also play a role in optimizing gut health by neutralizing free radicals and reducing oxidative stress.

Moreover, turmeric can enhance the production of bile, a substance crucial for the digestion and absorption of fats. This property makes turmeric a valuable ally for individuals with impaired fat digestion, providing relief from symptoms such as bloating and diarrhea.

Probiotics: Nature's Digestive Support

While not herbs per se, probiotics are essential players in maintaining a healthy digestive system. Probiotics are live bacteria and yeasts that confer numerous health benefits, particularly in promoting gut health and supporting digestion.

Research has shown that probiotics can modulate the gut microbiota by increasing the abundance of beneficial bacteria and suppressing harmful ones. This symbiotic relationship between humans and these "good bacteria" promotes digestion, boosts nutrient absorption, strengthens the gut barrier, and modulates immune responses.

Probiotics, such as Lactobacillus acidophilus and Bifidobacterium bifidum, have shown promise in managing digestive disorders such as diarrhea, constipation, and lactose intolerance. Additionally, probiotics may alleviate symptoms associated with inflammatory bowel disease and reduce the risk of complications due to their anti-inflammatory and immunomodulatory properties.

In recent years, modern research has shed light on the efficacy of various herbs in promoting digestive health. Peppermint, ginger, turmeric, and the use of probiotics have demonstrated promising results in managing various digestive disorders, ranging from IBS to GERD.

By understanding the active compounds and mechanisms of action behind these herbs, we can harness nature's potential to foster digestive harmony. With ongoing scientific exploration, these herbs and their derivatives may pave the way for new therapeutic approaches, improving the lives of those suffering from digestive ailments.

Chapter 6: Nervous System Support with Herbs

In our fast-paced, modern world, our nervous systems often bear the brunt of daily stressors. From work pressures to personal responsibilities, it's crucial to prioritize the well-being of our nervous system. Fortunately, nature offers us a wealth of medicinal herbs that can provide nurturing support and restore balance to our nervous system. In this chapter, we will explore a range of herbs renowned for their powerful effects on neurological health. By incorporating these herbs into our lives, we can promote relaxation, enhance cognitive function, and foster a sense of overall tranquility.

1. Chamomile: Nature's Calming Elixir

Chamomile, a small daisy-like flower, has long been cherished for its calming properties. This herb contains apigenin, a compound that binds to certain receptors in the brain, reducing anxiety and promoting relaxation. Consuming chamomile tea before bed has been shown to improve sleep quality and alleviate symptoms of insomnia. Additionally, chamomile possesses anti-inflammatory properties, helping to soothe tense muscles and reduce headaches associated with stress.

2. Ashwagandha: The Adaptogen Wonder

Ashwagandha is an ancient Ayurvedic herb used for centuries to combat stress and promote overall well-being. This adaptogenic herb supports the adrenal glands, enabling our bodies to better manage stressors. Numerous studies have shown that ashwagandha helps reduce cortisol levels, the stress hormone, enabling us to navigate challenging situations with renewed resilience. Ashwagandha also contains compounds that enhance brain function, improving memory, attention, and overall cognitive performance.

3. Valerian Root: The Herbal Tranquilizer

Valerian root has a long history as a natural sedative, helping to calm anxiety and promote relaxation. It contains valerenic acid, a compound that increases the levels of gamma-aminobutyric acid (GABA) in the brain. GABA is an inhibitory neurotransmitter that helps calm neural activity and induce a state of tranquility. Valerian root is often used as a sleep aid, as it effectively reduces the time it takes to fall asleep and enhances sleep quality. It is a widely used alternative to conventional medications for individuals suffering from insomnia or anxiety-related sleep disturbances.

4. Lavender: A Fragrant Remedy for Nerves

Lavender, with its delightful floral scent, possesses calming properties that have been revered throughout history. Inhaling lavender essential oil or steeping lavender flowers in tea can induce a calming effect by reducing anxiety and promoting relaxation.

Scientific studies have shown that lavender interacts with the same brain receptors as certain anti-anxiety medications but without the potential for side effects. Additionally, lavender aromatherapy can improve sleep quality, making it a valuable tool in combating insomnia.

5. St. John's Wort: A Natural Antidepressant

St. John's Wort is a famous flowering herb widely used as a natural remedy for depression and mood disorders. This herb contains hypericin and hyperforin, compounds that increase the levels of serotonin, dopamine, and norepinephrine in the brain. These neurotransmitters play a vital role in regulating mood, and low levels are associated with depression and anxiety. Multiple clinical trials have demonstrated the effectiveness of St. John's Wort in alleviating the symptoms of mild to moderate depression, making it a valuable option for those seeking natural alternatives to conventional antidepressants.

6. Ginseng: Energize and Elevate

Ginseng, a staple of traditional Chinese medicine, is revered for its ability to enhance mental clarity, focus, and overall cognitive function. This adaptogenic herb helps the body adapt to stress, improving physical and mental performance. Ginseng stimulates the release of neurotransmitters, particularly dopamine and norepinephrine, improving memory, concentration, and mental agility. It is commonly used to combat fatigue, increase energy levels, and support overall cognitive health.

7. Lemon Balm: Nature's Uplifting Herb

Lemon balm, also known as Melissa officinalis, is a lemon-scented herb that has been used since ancient times as a mood enhancer and relaxant. Lemon balm contains rosmarinic acid, which promotes a sense of calmness and well-being. It also possesses antiviral properties, making it beneficial in treating cold sores caused by the herpes simplex virus. Consuming lemon balm tea or including the herb in culinary preparations can help reduce anxiety, improve cognitive function, and elevate mood.

The nervous system plays a crucial role in our overall well-being, and prioritizing its support is essential in our modern lives. Incorporating herbs that promote relaxation, reduce anxiety, and improve cognitive function can have a profound impact on our mental and physical health. From chamomile and ashwagandha to valerian root and ginseng, nature provides us with a diverse array of herbs that assist in maintaining nervous system equilibrium. By harnessing the power of these herbs, we can embark on a journey towards enhanced tranquility, mental clarity, and overall well-being.

Calming Herbs: Anxiety and Stress Relief

In today's fast-paced world, anxiety and stress have become all too common. We find ourselves constantly juggling multiple responsibilities, struggling to meet deadlines, and striving for perfection in every aspect of our lives. This relentless pressure often takes a toll on our mental health, leaving us feeling overwhelmed, anxious, and stressed.

Fortunately, nature has provided us with a treasure trove of remedies to combat these modern-day anxieties. Calming herbs have been used for centuries to ease tension, promote relaxation, and restore emotional balance. In this chapter, we will explore some of the most effective herbs for anxiety and stress relief, unveiling their powerful benefits and revealing how you can incorporate them into your daily routine to find tranquility in a hectic world.

1. Chamomile: Nature's Gentle Sedative

Chamomile, with its delicate flowers and sweet aroma, is renowned for its calming properties. It has been used since ancient times to alleviate anxiety, promote restful sleep, and soothe frayed nerves. Chamomile contains compounds such as apigenin and luteolin, which interact with the brain's receptors to induce relaxation and reduce feelings of anxiety.

One of the most popular ways to consume chamomile is in the form of tea. Infuse a tablespoon of dried chamomile flowers in a cup of hot water for 5-10 minutes, then strain and enjoy. Sip this aromatic brew before bedtime to promote a peaceful night's sleep and help soothe anxiety.

2. Lavender: A Fragrant Remedy for Stress Relief

Lavender, with its vibrant purple flowers and enchanting scent, is often hailed as one of the ultimate stress-relieving herbs. Its aroma has an immediate calming effect, reducing feelings of restlessness and tension. Lavender contains compounds like linalool and linalyl acetate that interact with the nervous system to produce sedative effects.

To harness the benefits of lavender, consider using an essential oil diffuser to fill your living space with its soothing scent. You can also add a few drops of lavender essential oil to your bathwater, creating a luxurious and calming soak. Alternatively, dab a drop of lavender oil on your pulse points or pillow before bed to promote tranquility and a good night's sleep.

3. Lemon Balm: Nature's Antidepressant

Lemon balm, also known as Melissa officinalis, is an herb known for its uplifting and calming effects on the mind. It has been used for centuries to ease nervousness, promote relaxation, and alleviate symptoms of depression. Lemon balm contains compounds like rosmarinic acid and flavonoids that help boost mood and reduce anxiety.

You can make a refreshing lemon balm tea by steeping a handful of fresh leaves in hot water for 5-7 minutes. This delicious herbal tea can be enjoyed throughout the day to keep stress at bay. If you prefer a more concentrated form, lemon balm tinctures or capsules are readily available at health food stores.

4. Ashwagandha: The Ayurvedic Stress Buster

Ashwagandha, an ancient Ayurvedic herb, is often referred to as an adaptogen, meaning it helps the body adapt to stressors and restore balance. It has been used for centuries to reduce anxiety, enhance resilience, and promote overall well-being. Ashwagandha contains active compounds like withanolides that regulate cortisol levels, the stress hormone, leading to a calmer mind and increased mental clarity.

Ashwagandha can be consumed as a powder, capsule, or tincture. Mix a teaspoon of ashwagandha powder into warm milk or water and consume it before bedtime for a restful sleep. Regular use of ashwagandha over time can help modulate stress responses and provide long-term relief from anxiety.

5. Passionflower: Nature's Tranquilizer

Passionflower, with its intricate purple and white blossoms, is a powerful herb known for its anxiety-reducing properties. It contains compounds like flavonoids and alkaloids that enhance the production of gamma-aminobutyric acid (GABA), a neurotransmitter that promotes relaxation and calmness. Passionflower is particularly effective in reducing generalized anxiety disorder symptoms and improving sleep quality.

To enjoy the benefits of passionflower, brew a teaspoon of dried passionflower leaves in a cup of hot water for 10-15 minutes. This soothing tea can be consumed up to three times a day or before bedtime to induce relaxation and combat anxiety.

6. Valerian Root: Nature's Sedative

Valerian root, with its pungent aroma and gnarled appearance, has been used for centuries as a natural sleep aid and anxiety reducer. It contains compounds like valerenic acid and valepotriates that act as sedatives, calming the central nervous system and promoting restful sleep. Valerian root is particularly effective for individuals experiencing insomnia or restlessness due to anxiety.

Valerian root can be consumed as a tea or taken in capsule form. Steep a tablespoon of dried valerian root in hot water for 10-15 minutes and drink before bedtime. It is important to note that valerian root can cause drowsiness, so avoid operating heavy machinery or driving after consumption.

Calming herbs offer a natural and holistic approach to combat anxiety and stress, providing an alternative to pharmaceutical interventions. While these herbs are generally safe for most individuals, it is essential to consult with a healthcare professional before incorporating them into your routine, especially if you are taking any medications or have pre-existing health conditions.

The journey towards tranquility and emotional well-being may require experimentation to find the right herbs and dosage that work best for you. Remember to indulge in self-care practices alongside herbal remedies, such as regular exercise, sufficient sleep, and spending time in nature, to further enhance their efficacy.

By embracing the power of nature's remedies, we can pave the way for a healthier, more balanced life, free from the clutches of anxiety and stress. So, take a moment to reconnect with the healing forces of the earth and embark on a path towards serenity, one herb at a time.

Herbs for Enhancing Sleep Quality

In today's fast-paced world, the importance of a good night's sleep cannot be overstated. Sleep is not just a period of rest; it is a vital process that rejuvenates our bodies, minds, and spirits. Yet, numerous factors can disrupt our sleep patterns, such as stress, excessive screen time, and poor lifestyle choices. Instead of relying on pharmaceutical sleep aids, many individuals are turning to natural alternatives to promote better sleep quality. In this chapter, we will explore the world of herbs known for their sleep-enhancing properties. From ancient remedies to modern science, we will delve into the benefits, usage, and precautions associated with these natural sleep aids.

Passionflower:

Passionflower, or Passiflora incarnata, is a plant native to North America that has been used for centuries to address sleep disturbances. This herb contains compounds that interact with certain neurotransmitters in the brain, promoting relaxation and reducing anxiety. As a result, passionflower can help individuals fall asleep faster and experience deeper, more restful sleep. It is available in various forms such as tea, capsules, or tinctures. However, it is important to note that passionflower may cause drowsiness, so it should not be used in combination with other sedatives or depressants.

Valerian Root:

Valerian root, derived from the Valeriana officinalis plant, is another herb renowned for its sleep-inducing properties. Its sedative effects are believed to be attributed to a compound called valerenic acid, which increases levels of gamma-aminobutyric acid (GABA) in the brain. GABA is a neurotransmitter that promotes relaxation and helps calm the nervous system. Valerian root is commonly consumed as a tea or in supplement form. While generally safe, some individuals may experience mild side effects such as headaches or stomach discomfort. Additionally, long-term use should be done under the guidance of a healthcare professional.

Chamomile:

Chamomile, known for its soothing aroma and delicate white flowers, is a well-known herb utilized for centuries to improve sleep quality. The dried flowers of the Matricaria chamomilla plant are typically steeped in hot water to create a calming tea. Chamomile contains several compounds with sedative properties, including apigenin. These compounds bind to specific receptors in the brain, promoting relaxation and sleepiness. Chamomile tea is widely available and can be consumed before bedtime to support a peaceful night's rest. However, individuals with ragweed allergies should exercise caution, as chamomile can trigger similar reactions.

Lavender:

Lavender, with its distinctive purple flowers and calming scent, has long been associated with relaxation and improved sleep. Research suggests that inhaling lavender essential oil may promote better sleep quality, reduce anxiety levels, and increase feelings of well-being. This versatile herb can be used in various forms, such as essential oil diffusers, pillow sprays, or herbal bath additives. Remember to dilute essential oils properly before use and conduct a patch test to ensure there are no adverse reactions.

Lemon Balm:

Lemon balm, or Melissa officinalis, is a lemon-scented herb that belongs to the mint family. Traditionally, lemon balm has been used to alleviate anxiety and insomnia. It contains compounds that inhibit the breakdown of GABA, leading to increased levels of this calming neurotransmitter in the brain. As a result, lemon balm can help reduce anxiety and promote sleep. This herb can be consumed as a tea or taken in supplement form. However, individuals on thyroid medication should consult with their healthcare provider before consuming lemon balm, as it may interact with certain medications.

California Poppy:

California poppy, or Eschscholzia californica, is a vibrant orange wildflower found along the West Coast of the United States. Native American tribes traditionally used it as a sedative and analgesic herb. California poppy contains alkaloids, such as californidine, which exert mild sedative effects on the nervous system. This herb is primarily consumed in tincture or capsule form. It is important to note that California poppy may cause drowsiness, so it should not be combined with other sedatives or used before operating machinery.

The use of herbs to enhance sleep quality has been practiced for centuries, with numerous traditional remedies being validated by modern scientific research.

Passionflower, valerian root, chamomile, lavender, lemon balm, and California poppy are just a few examples of the vast range of herbs available to support a restful night's sleep. While these herbs can be effective for many individuals, it is essential to approach their usage with caution.

Chapter 7: Herbal Allies for Immune System

In this chapter, we will delve into the fascinating world of herbal allies that can support and strengthen our immune system. Our immune system plays a vital role in protecting us from harmful pathogens, viruses, and other foreign invaders. However, in today's fast-paced and stressful world, it is easy for our immune system to become compromised, leaving us vulnerable to illnesses and infections.

Fortunately, nature provides us with an abundance of plants and herbs that can act as allies in bolstering our immune response. From potent antiviral herbs to adaptogens that help our bodies adapt to stress, these herbal allies can enhance our immune system's ability to defend us against pathogens effectively.

1. Echinacea (Echinacea purpurea)

Echinacea, often referred to as the "king of immune herbs," has long been used to support and strengthen the immune system. This powerful herb boosts our body's production of white blood cells, which are crucial for fighting off infections and viruses.

Not only does echinacea stimulate the immune system directly, but it also exhibits potent anti-inflammatory properties. This makes it an effective herb to support the immune system during times of acute illness, such as colds and flu. Echinacea can be consumed as a tincture or made into a comforting tea, both of which harness its immune-boosting benefits.

2. Astragalus (Astragalus membranaceus)

Astragalus, a herb native to China, has been used in traditional Chinese medicine for centuries to fortify the immune system and protect against respiratory infections. Its immune-boosting properties largely stem from its ability to enhance the activity of natural killer cells, a key component of the immune system's defense against viral infections.

Additionally, astragalus possesses powerful antioxidant and anti-inflammatory properties, both of which contribute to its immune-supportive effects. This herb can be consumed in tincture form, brewed into a tea, or even added to soups and stews for a nourishing boost.

3. Elderberry (Sambucus nigra)

Elderberry has gained immense popularity in recent years due to its remarkable antiviral properties. This delicious dark purple berry contains potent antioxidants called anthocyanins, which help to strengthen the immune system and protect against viral infections.

Studies have shown that elderberry can significantly reduce the duration and severity of cold and flu symptoms. It can be consumed as a syrup, tincture, or made into a delightful and immune-boosting elderberry tea.

4. Reishi Mushroom (Ganoderma lucidum)

Reishi mushroom, also known as the "mushroom of immortality," has been highly revered in traditional Chinese medicine for its immune-modulating properties. This adaptogenic mushroom helps to balance and strengthen the immune system, making it an excellent ally during times of immune imbalance or suppressed immunity.

Reishi is known for its ability to reduce inflammation, protect against oxidative stress, and enhance the activity of certain immune cells. It is often consumed in powdered form or as a tincture, or alternatively, incorporated into soups and broths to reap its immunological benefits.

5. Garlic (Allium sativum)

Garlic is not only a culinary staple but also a potent immune-boosting herb. Its immune-enhancing effects largely stem from the presence of a compound called allicin, which exhibits antimicrobial and antiviral properties.
In addition to supporting immune function, garlic also possesses cardioprotective properties, making it a valuable addition to a healthy lifestyle. Adding fresh garlic to your meals or consuming garlic supplements can help fortify your immune system against various infections.

6. Ashwagandha (Withania somnifera)

Ashwagandha, an ancient Ayurvedic herb, is classified as an adaptogen due to its ability to help the body adapt to stress and restore balance. Chronic stress weakens the immune system, making us more susceptible to infections and illnesses. Ashwagandha counteracts this by reducing the production of stress hormones and supporting a healthy stress response.

Furthermore, ashwagandha possesses immunomodulatory properties, meaning it helps balance and regulate the immune system. This herb can be consumed as a powder, extracted into a tincture, or even brewed into a soothing tea.

As we conclude this chapter on herbal allies for the immune system, it is essential to remember that maintaining a healthy lifestyle, including a balanced diet, regular exercise, and sufficient sleep, is crucial for optimal immune function. However, incorporating these herbal allies into your routine can provide an extra layer of support and help you navigate the challenges that come your way.

Whether it's echinacea, astragalus, elderberry, reishi mushroom, garlic, or ashwagandha, these incredible plants have been used for centuries to enhance the immune system's strength and resilience. Utilizing nature's gifts can help us better protect ourselves against a multitude of pathogens and maintain vibrant health throughout our lives.

Boosting Immunity Through Herbal Means

In today's fast-paced world, maintaining a strong and robust immune system is paramount to living a healthy and fulfilling life. Our immune system acts as a defense mechanism, protecting us from harmful pathogens and preventing diseases from taking hold. While there are various ways to bolster our immunity, herbal remedies have been used by ancient cultures for centuries and continue to hold great significance in promoting optimal health. In this chapter, we will delve into the world of herbal remedies and explore the plants that can help boost our immune system naturally.

The Power of Herbs

Herbs have been an integral part of traditional medicine systems such as Ayurveda, Traditional Chinese Medicine (TCM), and Indigenous healing practices for thousands of years. These herbal medicines are derived from different parts of plants, including leaves, stems, flowers, roots, or barks, and vary widely in their chemical compositions and effects on the body. What makes herbs particularly fascinating is their ability to support the immune system while addressing various underlying health issues holistically.

Echinacea: The Immune Superstar

Echinacea, also known as the purple coneflower, is one of the most widely recognized herbs for boosting immunity. Native to North America, this flowering plant has been used by Native American tribes for centuries to treat infections and wounds. Echinacea is renowned for its immune-stimulating properties, which can enhance our body's ability to fight off viruses and bacteria.

Research has shown that echinacea can increase the production of white blood cells, which are crucial for immune function. This herb also possesses anti-inflammatory properties, supporting the body's response to infections. Echinacea can be consumed in various forms such as teas, tinctures, capsules, or tablets, making it readily accessible for immune support.

Garlic: Nature's Antibiotic

Known as the "stinking rose," garlic not only adds flavor to our cuisine but also possesses incredible immune-boosting properties. Garlic contains a compound called allicin, which gives it its distinct smell and acts as a potent antimicrobial agent. Allicin has been shown to have antibacterial, antiviral, and antifungal properties, making garlic an effective natural antibiotic.

Regular consumption of garlic can help strengthen the immune system, making us less susceptible to common infections and even chronic diseases. Adding garlic to our meals or taking garlic supplements can significantly enhance our immune response and overall well-being.

Ginseng: The Adaptogen

Ginseng is a popular herb in TCM, renowned for its adaptogenic properties. Adaptogens are a unique class of herbs that help the body adapt to various stressors, boosting its resistance to physical, mental, and environmental challenges. This immune-boosting herb can enhance the body's ability to fight infections, reduce fatigue, and improve overall vitality.

Ginseng contains compounds called ginsenosides, which have been shown to modulate immune responses by enhancing the activity of natural killer cells and macrophages, key players in our body's defense mechanism. Consuming ginseng regularly can fortify our immune system and promote overall well-being, enabling us to navigate life's challenges with ease.

Turmeric: The Golden Spice

Turmeric, often referred to as the "golden spice," is a vibrant yellow root that has been a staple in Ayurveda for centuries. This potent herb contains a compound called curcumin, which possesses potent anti-inflammatory and antioxidant properties. Curcumin has been shown to reduce inflammation, support immune function, and protect against various chronic diseases.

Studies have highlighted curcumin's ability to modulate immune responses by stimulating the production of white blood cells and enhancing their activity. Additionally, turmeric's antioxidant properties help neutralize harmful free radicals, further supporting immune function. Incorporating turmeric into our diet or taking curcumin supplements can aid in boosting our immune system and promoting optimal health.

Astragalus: The Protector

Astragalus is a key herb in TCM that has been used for centuries to support the immune system and protect against various diseases. This herb contains compounds called astragalosides, which have been shown to enhance immune cell function and stimulate the production of antibodies, promoting a robust immune response.

Astragalus also possesses potent antioxidant properties that protect the body against oxidative stress, which can weaken the immune system. This herb is commonly consumed as a tea or in extract form and can be a valuable addition to our immune-boosting regimen.

In this chapter, we have explored the powerful potential of herbal remedies in boosting our immune system naturally. From echinacea to garlic, ginseng to turmeric, and astragalus, these herbs offer a wide array of benefits that can fortify our body's defense mechanism and support optimal health.

While herbal remedies can be effective in boosting immunity, it's important to note that they should be used as complementary tools alongside a healthy lifestyle, balanced nutrition, regular exercise, and adequate sleep. As always, it is advisable to consult with a healthcare professional before incorporating any new herbal remedies into your routine, especially if you have pre-existing health conditions or are taking medication.

By harnessing the power of these herbs, we can nourish our immune system and cultivate a resilient foundation for vibrant well-being. As we embrace the wisdom of ancient healing traditions, we embark on a journey towards a healthier, more immune-empowered life.

Common Cold and Flu Remedies

Welcome to Chapter 7 of our comprehensive guide to natural remedies and holistic approaches to common illnesses. In this chapter, we will focus on the ever-present companions of the chilly seasons - the common cold and flu. This chapter aims to provide you with a comprehensive understanding of these ailments, their causes, symptoms, prevention strategies, and natural remedies that can help alleviate symptoms and promote a speedy recovery.

Section 1: Understanding the Common Cold

1.1 What is the Common Cold?

The common cold, also known as acute viral rhinopharyngitis, is an upper respiratory tract infection caused by various viruses. It is the most prevalent infectious disease in humans, typically affecting adults an average of 2-3 times per year and children even more frequently. The common cold is primarily characterized by symptoms like runny or stuffy nose, cough, sneezing, sore throat, and mild fatigue.

1.2 Causes and Transmission

Various viruses can cause the common cold, with the rhinovirus being the most common culprit. Other viruses like coronaviruses, respiratory syncytial virus (RSV), and adenoviruses can also be responsible. Transmission occurs primarily through respiratory droplets released when an infected person coughs, sneezes, or talks. Touching contaminated surfaces and then touching the face can also spread the virus.

1.3 Prevention Strategies

Preventing the common cold often revolves around practicing good hygiene habits. This includes frequently washing hands, avoiding close contact with infected individuals, and maintaining a healthy lifestyle with a balanced diet, regular exercise, and sufficient sleep. Additionally, boosting the immune system through vitamin supplements, such as vitamin C and zinc, and maintaining overall good health can also help prevent common colds.

Section 2: Understanding the Flu

2.1 What is the Flu?

Influenza, commonly known as the flu, is a highly contagious viral infection caused by the influenza virus. Unlike the common cold, the flu is characterized by a sudden onset of symptoms including high fever, headache, muscle aches, fatigue, and respiratory issues.

2.2 Causes and Transmission

The flu is caused by specific strains of the influenza virus, with influenza A and B being the most common culprits. Like the common cold, transmission occurs through respiratory droplets expelled when infected individuals cough, sneeze, or talk. The flu virus can also survive on surfaces and infect individuals who touch these surfaces and then touch their face or mouth.

2.3 Prevention Strategies

Preventing the flu involves similar strategies as those used for preventing the common cold, such as practicing good hygiene, washing hands regularly, avoiding close contact with infected individuals, and getting vaccinated. The flu vaccine, although not always 100% effective, is still considered the best preventive measure available.

Section 3: Natural Remedies for Common Cold and Flu

3.1 Rest and Hydration

One of the most crucial aspects of treating the common cold and flu is providing the body with ample rest and hydration. Rest allows the immune system to focus on fighting the infection, while staying hydrated helps thin mucus, soothe a sore throat, and prevent dehydration caused by fever.

3.2 Steam Inhalation

Steam inhalation can provide immense relief from nasal congestion and respiratory discomfort associated with the common cold and flu. By adding a few drops of eucalyptus or peppermint essential oil to hot water and inhaling the vapors, you can provide temporary relief and reduce congestion.

3.3 Saltwater Gargles

Gargling with warm saltwater can help soothe a sore throat caused by the common cold or flu. A homemade solution of ½ teaspoon salt dissolved in 8 ounces of warm water can be used several times a day to alleviate discomfort and inflammation.

3.4 Herbal Teas and Warm Broths

Consuming warm herbal teas, such as chamomile, ginger, or echinacea, can provide relief from symptoms, reduce inflammation, and give your immune system a gentle boost. Similarly, warm broths, such as chicken soup, can help soothe a sore throat and provide nourishment to the body.

3.5 Nasal Irrigation

Using a neti pot or saline nasal spray can help remove excess mucus and relieve nasal congestion. Be sure to follow proper instructions and use sterile water or saline solution.

In this chapter, we explored the common cold and flu, including their causes, transmission methods, prevention strategies, and natural remedies to alleviate symptoms. By following proper hygiene practices, adopting a healthy lifestyle, and utilizing natural remedies, you can empower yourself to combat these seasonal ailments effectively. Remember, maintaining a strong immune system and seeking medical advice when warranted are crucial steps in promoting a quick recovery.

Herbs with Antimicrobial Properties

Throughout history, humans have relied on various natural remedies to combat infections and illnesses. Long before the advent of modern medicine, our ancestors harnessed the power of plants and herbs to treat wounds, fight infections, and alleviate symptoms. With the rise of antibiotic resistance and the limitations of synthetic drugs, the interest in natural alternatives has resurged. In this chapter, we will explore the fascinating world of herbs with antimicrobial properties, their historical significance, and their potential applications in modern medicine. Join us as we embark on a journey through time and nature's pharmacy.

Ancient Wisdom: Historical Significance of Herbs

Herbs have long been regarded as natural healers, with antimicrobial activities discovered by our ancestors through trial and error. Many ancient civilizations, including the Egyptians, Greeks, and Chinese, relied heavily on plant-based medicines to treat various ailments. These traditional practices, passed down through generations, have served as the foundation for modern herbal medicine.

One of the earliest documented examples of the use of herbs with antimicrobial properties can be found in ancient Egypt. The Ebers Papyrus, dating back over 3,500 years, lists several plant-based remedies for infectious diseases. Garlic, for instance, was used to treat parasitic infections, while myrrh was recognized for its wound healing properties. These ancient civilizations understood the power carried by nature's remedies, and their knowledge formed the basis for centuries of exploration and discovery.

Exploring the Science: The Antimicrobial Mechanisms of Herbs

While our ancestors may not have had a complete understanding of the scientific principles behind herbs' antimicrobial properties, modern research has shed light on their mechanisms of action. Many herbs contain a myriad of phytochemicals, compounds responsible for their biological activities. It is these phytochemicals that determine the ability of herbs to defend against microorganisms.

Several classes of phytochemicals found in herbs possess antimicrobial properties. Phenols, such as thymol and eugenol, disrupt the cell membranes of microorganisms, leading to their destruction. Polyphenols, including flavonoids and tannins, inhibit the growth of bacteria by interfering with their metabolic processes. Terpenoids, another group of phytochemicals, exhibit antimicrobial activity by disrupting cell signaling and enzymatic pathways in microorganisms.

Herbs That Pack a Punch: Antimicrobial Powerhouses

1. Garlic (Allium sativum):
With a rich history dating back over 5,000 years, garlic is renowned for its antimicrobial properties. Allicin, the active compound in garlic, has been found to possess broad-spectrum antimicrobial activity. It can inhibit the growth of both Gram-positive and Gram-negative bacteria, as well as fungi and viruses. Garlic's efficacy against various pathogens, including antibiotic-resistant strains, has led to its promising applications in modern medicine.

2. Oregano (Origanum vulgare):
Apart from its culinary uses, oregano has gained significant attention for its potent antimicrobial activities. Carvacrol, the primary active compound found in oregano, has demonstrated strong bactericidal properties against multiple drug-resistant strains, including Methicillin-resistant Staphylococcus aureus (MRSA). Its ability to disrupt bacterial cell membranes makes it a promising candidate for the development of new antibiotics.

3. Tea Tree (Melaleuca alternifolia):
Indigenous to Australia, the tea tree has a long history of medicinal use by Aboriginal communities. Its essential oil exhibits broad-spectrum antimicrobial activity, making it an effective remedy for various infections. Terpinen-4-ol, the primary active constituent in tea tree oil, has demonstrated potent antibacterial, antifungal, and antiviral properties. This versatile herb continues to find applications in skincare, wound healing, and oral health.

4. Turmeric (Curcuma longa):

Widely known for its vibrant color and culinary uses, turmeric is also a potent medicinal herb. The active compound, curcumin, possesses significant antimicrobial and anti-inflammatory activities. It inhibits the growth of various bacteria, including Helicobacter pylori, which causes gastric ulcers. Curcumin's potential in combating antibiotic-resistant bacteria is an area of active research, holding promise for future therapeutic interventions.

5. Neem (Azadirachta indica):

Native to the Indian subcontinent, neem has been used for centuries in traditional Ayurvedic medicine. It exhibits a wide range of pharmacological activities, including antimicrobial and antiparasitic effects. The neem tree's extracts and oil contain compounds such as nimbin and azadirachtin, which have been shown to inhibit the growth of bacteria, fungi, and protozoa. Neem-based products continue to be explored as potential alternatives to synthetic drugs for various infectious diseases.

Unleashing the Potential: Herbs for Modern Medicine

The growing concern of antibiotic resistance has necessitated the exploration of alternative therapeutic options. Herbs with antimicrobial properties offer promising avenues for the development of novel treatments. However, it is important to approach this potential with caution and thorough scientific scrutiny.

Harnessing the antimicrobial power of herbs requires rigorous research, clinical trials, and standardized formulations. Integration of herbal medicine into conventional healthcare systems requires broad collaboration between scientists, herbalists, and medical professionals. By capitalizing on nature's pharmacy and the wisdom of our ancestors, we can uncover new strategies to combat infectious diseases in the era of antibiotic resistance.

In this chapter, we have traversed the historical significance, scientific mechanisms, and potential applications of herbs with antimicrobial properties. These natural healers offer a glimpse into the rich tapestry of traditional medicine that has been passed down through generations. As the world faces the daunting challenge of antibiotic resistance, exploring the therapeutic potential of herbs becomes increasingly important. By combining ancient wisdom with modern scientific methodologies, we can unlock nature's secrets and pave the way for innovative solutions to microbial infections.

Autoimmune Conditions and Herbal Management

In recent years, there has been a growing interest in the use of herbal remedies for managing autoimmune conditions. Autoimmune diseases are characterized by an overactive immune response, whereby the immune system mistakenly attacks healthy cells and tissues in the body. These conditions can have a profound impact on a person's overall well-being, as they often result in chronic inflammation, pain, and a range of debilitating symptoms. While conventional medical treatments are typically aimed at suppressing the immune system, herbal management offers a more holistic approach, focusing on modulating the immune response and reducing inflammation. In this chapter, we will explore various herbal remedies that have shown promising results in managing autoimmune conditions.

Herbal Approaches to Autoimmune Management

Herbal medicine has been used for centuries in traditional healing systems such as Ayurveda and Traditional Chinese Medicine (TCM). These ancient practices recognize the body's innate ability to heal itself and aim to restore balance and harmony. Many herbs used in these systems possess immunomodulatory and anti-inflammatory properties, making them potentially beneficial for individuals with autoimmune conditions.

One such herb is Turmeric (Curcuma longa), a bright yellow spice commonly used in Indian cuisine. A key component of turmeric, curcumin, has been extensively studied for its anti-inflammatory effects. Research has shown that curcumin can inhibit several inflammatory pathways that are implicated in autoimmune diseases. Additionally, curcumin has been found to modulate immune cells, suppressing their activity when it is excessive and stimulating them when it is deficient. Incorporating turmeric into the diet or taking curcumin supplements may help reduce inflammation and alleviate symptoms in autoimmune conditions such as rheumatoid arthritis and multiple sclerosis.

Another herb that has gained attention in autoimmune management is Boswellia (Boswellia serrata), also known as Indian frankincense. The resin extract from the Boswellia tree has been a staple in Ayurvedic medicine for centuries due to its potent anti-inflammatory properties. Studies suggest that boswellic acids, the active compounds in Boswellia, can inhibit pro-inflammatory enzymes and modulate immune responses. This herb has shown promise in managing conditions like rheumatoid arthritis, ulcerative colitis, and asthma.

The adaptogenic herb Ashwagandha (Withania somnifera) has also garnered interest in the realm of autoimmune management. Adaptogens are a unique class of herbs that help the body adapt to stress and restore balance. Ashwagandha, in particular, has been shown to modulate the immune system by regulating the production of pro-inflammatory and anti-inflammatory cytokines. This herb's ability to reduce the excessive immune response makes it potentially beneficial for managing autoimmune conditions such as psoriasis, lupus, and Hashimoto's thyroiditis.

Herbal Formulations and Combinations

While individual herbs have their merits, herbal formulations and combinations often yield more comprehensive and synergistic effects. Many traditional herbal blends have been used for centuries to address autoimmune conditions effectively.

One significant example is Triphala, an Ayurvedic formulation consisting of three fruits: Amalaki (Emblica officinalis), Bibhitaki (Terminalia bellirica), and Haritaki (Terminalia chebula). Triphala is renowned for its powerful antioxidant and immune-modulating properties. It has been shown to enhance immune function, reduce inflammation, and promote tissue regeneration. These properties make Triphala a valuable herbal solution for autoimmune conditions like rheumatoid arthritis, ulcerative colitis, and systemic lupus erythematosus.

Another herbal combination worth considering is the popular TCM formula known as Xiao Yao San or "Free and Easy Wanderer." This blend incorporates herbs such as Bupleurum (Bupleurum chinense), Peony (Paeonia lactiflora), and Chinese Skullcap (Scutellaria baicalensis), among others. Xiao Yao San works by harmonizing the liver and spleen, which are central organs in TCM associated with emotional health and immune function. By reducing liver stagnation and tonifying the spleen, this formula may help alleviate symptoms of autoimmune conditions linked to emotional stress, such as psoriasis, eczema, and vitiligo.

Safety and Precautions

While herbal management can offer promising benefits for autoimmune conditions, it is vital to use them under the guidance of a qualified healthcare professional. Some herbs may interact with medications or have potential side effects, especially in high doses. Individuals with autoimmune conditions often have complex health profiles, and a tailored approach is crucial to ensure safety and effectiveness.

Autoimmune conditions present complex challenges that require holistic management approaches. Herbal medicine offers a wealth of potential solutions by harnessing the immune-modulating and anti-inflammatory properties of various plants. Turmeric, Boswellia, Ashwagandha, and Triphala are just a few examples of herbs that have shown promise in managing autoimmune conditions. However, it is essential to remember that individual responses may vary, and consultation with a healthcare professional is paramount. By combining the power of ancient herbal knowledge with modern scientific understanding, a comprehensive approach to autoimmune management can be achieved, promoting better quality of life for those affected by these conditions.

Chapter 8: Herbs for Musculoskeletal Wellness

In our modern lifestyle, where sedentary habits and desk-bound jobs are the norm, musculoskeletal issues have become increasingly common. Whether it's back pain, joint stiffness, or general muscle fatigue, many people find themselves grappling with these challenges on a regular basis. Fortunately, traditional herbal remedies can offer effective and natural solutions to support musculoskeletal wellness. In this chapter, we will explore some key herbs and their benefits in maintaining healthy muscles, bones, and joints.

Understanding Musculoskeletal Health

Before delving into the specific herbs, let's first understand the essential components of musculoskeletal health. The musculoskeletal system comprises bones, muscles, tendons, ligaments, and joints, all working together harmoniously to facilitate movement, stability, and protection. However, various factors such as age, injury, inflammation, and nutritional deficiencies can disrupt this delicate balance, leading to discomfort and reduced functionality.

Herbs for Musculoskeletal Wellness

1. Turmeric (Curcuma longa)

Turmeric, a vibrant yellow spice commonly found in curry dishes, has been used for centuries in traditional medicine due to its potent anti-inflammatory properties. The active compound, curcumin, helps reduce inflammation in the joints, making it a valuable herb for managing conditions like arthritis. Regular consumption of turmeric or its extract may alleviate joint pain and stiffness, improving overall musculoskeletal well-being.

2. Ginger (Zingiber officinale)

Renowned for its digestive benefits, ginger also offers remarkable support for musculoskeletal health. Ginger acts as a natural analgesic and anti-inflammatory agent, reducing muscle pain, swelling, and inflammation. Incorporating ginger into your diet, whether in its fresh form, as a soothing tea, or in powdered supplement form, can help alleviate discomfort from musculoskeletal issues.

3. Boswellia (Boswellia serrata)

Derived from the resin of the Boswellia tree, boswellia extract has been traditionally used to support joint health and mobility. It contains potent anti-inflammatory compounds, such as boswellic acids, which inhibit the production of pro-inflammatory enzymes. By reducing inflammation, boswellia may improve muscle and joint function, making it a great choice for those seeking natural muscle and joint support.

4. Devil's Claw (Harpagophytum procumbens)

Native to the African continent, devil's claw has long been used in traditional medicine to alleviate musculoskeletal discomfort. Its active ingredients, known as harpagosides, possess anti-inflammatory and analgesic properties. Devil's claw is particularly useful in managing various musculoskeletal issues like arthritis, muscle pain, and even lower back pain.

5. Arnica (Arnica montana)

Arnica, a widely recognized herb in herbal medicine, offers effective relief from musculoskeletal injuries, sprains, and bruises. It possesses anti-inflammatory and pain-relieving properties that promote healing and reduce swelling. Arnica-based creams or salves can be applied topically to the affected area, providing quick relief from discomfort caused by muscle strain or joint injuries.

6. White Willow Bark (Salix alba)

White willow bark, derived from the tree of the same name, has been used for centuries as a natural remedy for pain and inflammation. Its active compound, salicin, is converted within the body into salicylic acid, similar to the active component found in aspirin. This makes white willow bark an effective natural alternative for managing musculoskeletal pain, particularly in conditions like osteoarthritis.

7. Comfrey (Symphytum officinale)

Comfrey, a perennial herb native to Europe, offers impressive benefits for musculoskeletal health. It contains allantoin, a constituent known for its ability to stimulate cell regeneration, promoting faster healing of bones, ligaments, and tendons. Comfrey-based creams or ointments can be applied externally to the affected area, aiding in the recovery from sports injuries or joint sprains.

Maintaining musculoskeletal wellness is vital for a healthy and active lifestyle. The herbs mentioned above, such as turmeric, ginger, boswellia, devil's claw, arnica, white willow bark, and comfrey, offer natural and effective support for managing musculoskeletal issues. However, it is important to consult with a healthcare professional or herbalist before incorporating any new herbs or supplements into your routine, especially if you have pre-existing medical conditions or are currently taking medication. Remember, when it comes to musculoskeletal health, prevention and holistic care are key to long-term well-being.

Herbal Approaches to Muscle Relaxation

In today's fast-paced and stressful world, muscle tension and tightness have become common complaints among individuals of all ages. Whether it is due to long hours spent at a desk, physical exertion, or sports-related injuries, finding effective methods to relax and relieve muscle tension is essential for maintaining optimal health and well-being. While there are various conventional methods available, many individuals are turning to herbal approaches for muscle relaxation as a safe and natural alternative. In this chapter, we will explore the power of herbal remedies in addressing muscle tension and fatigue, providing an insight into the most popular and effective herbs.

Understanding Muscle Tension:

Muscle tension occurs when muscles contract and resist relaxing, leading to discomfort and limited mobility. It can be a result of physical strain, strenuous exercise, poor posture, stress, or underlying medical conditions. When left untreated, chronic muscle tension can lead to further complications, such as headaches, neck pain, and decreased flexibility. Herbal remedies offer a holistic approach to alleviate muscle tension by targeting the root cause and promoting relaxation.

The Healing Power of Herbalism:

Herbal medicine has been used for centuries across various cultures to address a wide range of health conditions. Herbs contain chemical compounds that have therapeutic effects on the body, and their natural properties make them a gentle yet potent solution for muscle relaxation. Unlike pharmaceutical drugs, herbal remedies often have fewer side effects and provide a more holistic approach to healing.

Chamomile:

Chamomile, known for its calming properties, is a popular herb used in traditional medicine for muscle relaxation. The flowers of the chamomile plant contain compounds that possess anti-inflammatory and antispasmodic properties. Chamomile can help soothe muscle tension, reduce inflammation, and promote relaxation. It can be consumed as a tea or applied topically in the form of essential oil or infused oil for a relaxing massage.

Lavender:

Lavender is a versatile herb renowned for its soothing aroma and muscle relaxation properties. It contains compounds that act as natural muscle relaxants and pain relievers. Inhalation of lavender essential oil can help calm the mind and body, reducing muscle tension caused by stress. Additionally, lavender oil can be used in a warm bath or applied topically to ease muscle soreness and aid in relaxation.

Valerian Root:

Valerian root has been used for centuries as a herbal sleep aid due to its calming effect on the nervous system. This herb contains compounds that act as muscle relaxants, making it beneficial for alleviating muscle tension and promoting healthy sleep. Valerian root is available in various forms, including teas, capsules, and tinctures, making it easily accessible for those seeking natural muscle relaxation.

Passionflower:

Passionflower is a gentle herb known for its muscle relaxation properties and its ability to alleviate anxiety and stress. It contains compounds that help reduce muscle spasms, making it an effective remedy for muscle tension caused by physical or emotional stress. Passionflower can be consumed as a tea, taken in capsule form, or used as a tincture, offering versatility and convenience.

Arnica:

Arnica is a herb widely used topically as a cream or gel for muscle relaxation and pain relief. It possesses anti-inflammatory properties that help reduce swelling and pain associated with muscle tension, sprains, and bruises. Arnica can be applied directly to the affected area to provide immediate relief and accelerate the healing process.

St. John's Wort:

St. John's Wort is a well-known herb used for its antidepressant properties, but it also offers benefits in muscle relaxation. This herb contains compounds that help calm the nervous system, reduce muscle spasms, and promote overall relaxation. St. John's Wort can be consumed as a tea or taken in capsule form, making it a versatile option for muscle tension relief.

Turmeric:

Turmeric is a vibrant yellow herb widely used in traditional medicine for its anti-inflammatory properties. It contains curcumin, a compound known for reducing pain and inflammation. Turmeric can be consumed as a spice in food or taken in capsule form to reduce muscle tension caused by inflammation or injury.

Herbal approaches to muscle relaxation offer a natural and holistic alternative to conventional treatments. The power of herbal medicine lies in its ability to address the root cause of muscle tension while promoting overall well-being. Chamomile, lavender, valerian root, passionflower, arnica, St. John's Wort, and turmeric are just a few examples of the many herbs available for muscle relaxation. Integrating herbal remedies into your daily routine can help you achieve optimal muscle function, relieve tension, and enhance your quality of life. Explore the world of herbalism and experience the profound benefits of nature's healing touch.

Complementary Herbal Therapies for Arthritis

Arthritis is a common degenerative condition that affects millions of individuals worldwide. It is characterized by joint inflammation, pain, stiffness, and reduced mobility. While conventional medical treatments for arthritis often involve the use of anti-inflammatory drugs and painkillers, many individuals explore complementary herbal therapies to manage their symptoms and improve their quality of life. In this chapter, we will delve into some of the most widely used herbal remedies for arthritis, exploring their potential benefits, safety, and relevant scientific evidence.

1. Turmeric:

Turmeric, derived from the rhizome of Curcuma longa, has been used for centuries in Ayurvedic and traditional Chinese medicine for its anti-inflammatory properties. The active compound in turmeric, known as curcumin, has demonstrated significant potential in reducing joint pain, swelling, and stiffness associated with various forms of arthritis.

Numerous studies suggest that curcumin possesses powerful antioxidant and anti-inflammatory effects, which can potentially inhibit inflammatory pathways involved in arthritis. However, it is worth noting that the bioavailability of curcumin is relatively low, and consuming it with black pepper or in lipid-based formulations may enhance its absorption and effectiveness.

2. Ginger:

Ginger, derived from the Zingiber officinale plant, is another popular herbal remedy used for arthritis. Ginger contains compounds known as gingerols, which possess anti-inflammatory and analgesic properties. These compounds may help alleviate pain and reduce inflammation in arthritic joints.

Several clinical trials have demonstrated the benefits of ginger in reducing joint pain and swelling, especially in individuals with osteoarthritis and rheumatoid arthritis. Ginger can be consumed fresh, as a tea, or as a supplement. However, ginger may interact with certain medications, so it is essential to consult with a healthcare professional before adding ginger to your arthritis management plan.

3. Green Tea:

Green tea, derived from the leaves of Camellia sinensis, is rich in polyphenols and antioxidants. These bioactive compounds, especially epigallocatechin-3-gallate (EGCG), have shown promising anti-inflammatory effects and cartilage-protecting properties.

One study investigating the potential benefits of green tea extract in arthritis reported reduced disease activity and improved symptoms in individuals with rheumatoid arthritis. However, more research is needed to determine the optimal dosage and long-term effects of green tea consumption as a complementary therapy for arthritis.

4. Boswellia:

Boswellia serrata, also known as Indian frankincense, has long been used in traditional medicine for its anti-inflammatory properties. The main active compounds in Boswellia, known as boswellic acids, have been shown to inhibit the production of inflammatory molecules that contribute to arthritis progression.

Multiple studies suggest that Boswellia extract may improve pain, joint stiffness, and functional ability in individuals with osteoarthritis and rheumatoid arthritis. Moreover, Boswellia has demonstrated a good safety profile, making it an appealing herbal therapy for arthritis management.

5. Devil's Claw:

Devil's claw (Harpagophytum procumbens) is a plant native to southern Africa, traditionally used for its analgesic and anti-inflammatory properties. It contains iridoid glycosides, including harpagoside, which is thought to be responsible for its potential benefits in arthritis.

Clinical trials investigating the efficacy of devil's claw in osteoarthritis have reported reduced pain and improved functional scores. However, more research is necessary to establish its long-term safety and potential interactions with other medications.

6. Cat's Claw:

Cat's claw (Uncaria tomentosa) is a woody vine native to the Amazon rainforest. It is known for its immunomodulatory properties, and its use in arthritis is primarily attributed to its potential to reduce inflammation and regulate the immune response.

Preliminary studies have demonstrated promising results regarding cat's claw's ability to reduce joint pain and swelling in rheumatoid arthritis patients. However, its safety and optimal dosage in long-term use require further investigation.

The use of complementary herbal therapies for managing arthritis symptoms is widely practiced, with an increasing body of scientific evidence supporting their potential benefits. However, it is crucial to acknowledge that these herbal remedies should not replace conventional medical treatments, but rather act as adjunct therapies. Before incorporating any herbal remedy into your arthritis management plan, it is vital to consult with a qualified healthcare professional. This will allow for a comprehensive evaluation of your condition, potential drug interactions, optimal dosage, and possible side effects.

The field of complementary herbal therapies for arthritis is continuously evolving, and further research is needed to shed light on their mechanisms, effectiveness, and long-term safety. Nonetheless, the exploration of these natural options offers hope for individuals seeking additional support in managing their arthritis symptoms and improving their overall well-being.

Chapter 9: Skin Conditions and Herbal Treatments

The skin is the largest organ in our body and plays a crucial role in protecting us from external elements. However, it is also prone to various conditions, ranging from minor irritations to chronic diseases. This chapter explores some common skin conditions and the herbal treatments that have been used for centuries to alleviate their symptoms and promote overall skin health. We will delve into the fascinating world of botanical remedies, their historical use, and their effectiveness in treating various skin disorders.

Acne:

Acne is a bothersome condition that affects individuals of all ages, especially during puberty. It occurs when hair follicles become clogged with dead skin cells and excessive oil production. Herbal treatments for acne have gained popularity due to their potential effectiveness and minimal side effects. One such herb is tea tree oil, derived from the Australian native plant Melaleuca alternifolia. Tea tree oil possesses antibacterial and anti-inflammatory properties, making it an ideal choice for treating acne. Applying diluted tea tree oil topically can help unclog pores and reduce inflammation, effectively combating acne.

Psoriasis:

Psoriasis is a chronic autoimmune disorder that causes red, scaly patches on the skin. This condition can significantly impact an individual's quality of life due to its persistent nature. Herbal treatments for psoriasis often focus on reducing inflammation and promoting skin cell regeneration. Aloe vera, a succulent plant known for its soothing properties, has been used for centuries to treat various skin conditions. Applying aloe vera gel to affected areas can provide instant relief from itching and redness commonly associated with psoriasis.

Eczema:

Eczema, also known as atopic dermatitis, is a chronic skin condition characterized by itchy, inflamed patches. It is often aggravated by environmental factors, stress, and certain allergies. Herbal remedies for eczema aim to reduce irritation, moisturize the skin, and strengthen the skin barrier. Chamomile, a herb revered for its calming properties, can be brewed into a tea or used topically as a compress to alleviate eczema symptoms. The anti-inflammatory compounds found in chamomile can soothe irritated skin and promote healing.

Rosacea:

Rosacea is a common skin condition that primarily affects the face, causing redness, visible blood vessels, and small, pus-filled bumps. The exact cause of rosacea remains unknown, and its treatment typically involves managing symptoms. Many herbal remedies for rosacea focus on reducing inflammation and strengthening the skin's barrier function. Green tea, containing catechins and polyphenols, has been found to possess potent anti-inflammatory and antioxidant properties. Introducing green tea extracts or using green tea as a topical wash can help alleviate redness and reduce inflammation associated with rosacea.

Wound Healing:

Our skin's ability to heal wounds is paramount for our overall health and well-being. Herbal treatments that aid in wound healing have been utilized for centuries. Calendula, also known as marigold, has been widely used for its regenerative and antimicrobial properties. The flowers of this plant can be made into a salve or infused into an oil to enhance wound healing. Applying calendula-based products on wounds can accelerate the healing process, reduce scarring, and prevent infection.

Burns:

Burns can be painful and require proper care to promote faster healing. Herbal treatments for burns often focus on soothing the burn, reducing pain, and preventing infection. Aloe vera, with its cooling and moisturizing properties, is a popular choice for treating burn wounds. Applying pure aloe vera gel to the affected area can provide instant relief from pain and aid in the healing process. Additionally, lavender oil, known for its soothing aroma, possesses excellent antiseptic properties. Diluted lavender oil can be applied topically to burns to prevent infection and enhance healing.

The information presented in this chapter showcases the rich legacy of herbal treatments for various skin conditions. Herbal remedies have been utilized for centuries as alternative or complementary therapies, offering individuals a more holistic approach to skin health. While these botanical treatments can provide relief and support the healing process, it is essential to consult with a healthcare professional or licensed herbalist before embarking on any herbal treatment regimen to ensure safety and efficacy. Ultimately, the integration of traditional herbal knowledge with modern scientific research can pave the way for innovative treatments that benefit individuals with diverse skin conditions.

Herbs for Wound Healing and Scar Reduction

Wounds are a common occurrence in our everyday lives, ranging from minor cuts and scrapes to more severe injuries. While our bodies possess remarkable regenerative abilities, the healing process can be aided by various natural remedies, including the use of herbs. Throughout history, humans have relied on the healing properties of herbs to promote wound healing and minimize scarring. In this chapter, we will explore some of the most effective herbs for wound healing and scar reduction, their mechanisms of action, and how to incorporate them into your healing regimen. So, without further ado, let's delve into the world of nature's botanical healers.

1. Calendula (Calendula officinalis):

Calendula, also known as pot marigold, has been used for centuries for its remarkable wound-healing properties. It possesses anti-inflammatory, antibacterial, and antifungal properties, making it an invaluable herb for wound care. Calendula promotes tissue regeneration, reduces swelling, and prevents infection, thereby accelerating the healing process. Its high content of flavonoids and triterpenes helps stimulate collagen production, leading to minimization of scars. Topical application of calendula in the form of creams, ointments, or infused oils proves most effective.

2. Aloe Vera (Aloe barbadensis):

Aloe vera, often referred to as the "plant of immortality," has been revered for its healing properties for centuries. The gel obtained from its succulent leaves contains a rich blend of bioactive compounds that promote wound healing and reduce scarring. Aloe vera possesses antimicrobial properties, keeping wounds clean and free from infection. Moreover, it stimulates the production of collagen and elastin, vital components for healthy skin growth and reducing scar formation. Applying fresh aloe vera gel directly to the wound or using commercially available products can expedite healing and reduce scar visibility.

3. Gotu Kola (Centella asiatica):

For thousands of years, traditional Asian medicine has utilized gotu kola for its wound-healing capabilities. Its active compounds, such as triterpenoids and asiaticoside, enhance collagen synthesis, strengthen connective tissues, and improve blood circulation to the affected area. Gotu kola accelerates wound closure, reduces inflammation, and prevents excessive scar formation. It is available as an extract, cream, or ointment that can be applied topically to the wound for optimal healing results.

4. Lavender (Lavandula angustifolia):

Lavender, with its enchanting fragrance, possesses powerful healing properties that make it a popular choice for wound care. Its essential oil contains compounds like linalool and linalyl acetate, which have antimicrobial, anti-inflammatory, and analgesic properties. Lavender oil's ability to stimulate cell regeneration and promote collagen synthesis makes it effective for reducing scar formation. Applying diluted lavender essential oil topically or using lavender-infused creams can aid in wound healing and scar reduction, while also providing a soothing effect.

5. Comfrey (Symphytum officinale):

Comfrey, also known as "knit-bone," has been extensively used to heal wounds and fractures due to its remarkable ability to regenerate tissues. Allantoin, a compound found in comfrey, accelerates wound healing by stimulating cell proliferation and promoting the growth of new blood vessels. Comfrey also contains rosmarinic acid, which has anti-inflammatory properties, aiding in pain relief and reducing swelling. It can be applied as a poultice, salve, or cream to promote speedy wound closure and minimize scarring.

6. Chamomile (Matricaria chamomilla):

Chamomile, renowned for its calming properties, also possesses exceptional wound-healing abilities. Its essential oil and extracts contain potent anti-inflammatory and antioxidant compounds, such as bisabolol and chamazulene. These compounds reduce inflammation, prevent microbial growth, and support tissue regeneration. Chamomile's ability to inhibit collagenase, an enzyme responsible for breaking down collagen, helps prevent excessive scar formation. Topical application of chamomile-infused creams, oils, or chamomile tea compresses can promote wound healing and minimize scarring.

7. Rosehip (Rosa canina):

Rosehip, the fruit of the wild rose, is a powerhouse of skin-loving nutrients, including vitamins A, C, and E, all of which are essential for wound healing. Its high antioxidant content protects the skin from free radicals, prevents tissue damage, and supports collagen synthesis. Rosehip also contains essential fatty acids like linoleic acid, which has anti-inflammatory properties, promoting healthy skin regeneration and minimizing scars. Topical application of rosehip oil or creams can aid in wound healing and prevent the formation of unsightly scars.

In this chapter, we have explored some of nature's most potent herbs for wound healing and scar reduction. These herbs, including calendula, aloe vera, gotu kola, lavender, comfrey, chamomile, and rosehip, offer a natural and effective approach to enhance the healing process and minimize scarring. Whether applied directly to the wound or used in the form of creams, oils, or poultices, these herbs harness the power of nature to support the body's regenerative abilities. Integrating these herbs into your wound care routine can significantly enhance the healing process, leaving you with healthy, scar-free skin. Remember, nature offers us an abundance of botanical healers; it is up to us to tap into their potential and unlock their healing benefits.

Addressing Acne and Blemishes

Chapter 1: Understanding Acne and Blemishes

In today's beauty-conscious world, achieving clear and flawless skin is a common desire. However, for millions of individuals, acne and blemishes can become a frustrating and persistent obstacle on their path to achieving that goal. In this chapter, we will delve into the underlying causes of acne and blemishes, as well as explore their various types and manifestations.

1.1 The Science Behind Acne:

Acne, one of the most prevalent skin conditions, emerges when hair follicles become clogged with oil and dead skin cells. These obstructions provide the perfect breeding ground for bacteria, leading to an inflammatory response by the body. Hormonal fluctuations, particularly during adolescence, play a significant role in triggering acne outbreaks. Nonetheless, factors like genetics, stress, and certain medications can also contribute to acne formation.

1.2 Types of Acne:

Acne manifests itself in various forms, each with its unique characteristics. The most common types include:

"

1.2.1 Whiteheads and Blackheads:

Whiteheads and blackheads are non-inflammatory acne lesions. Whiteheads occur when sebum and dead skin cells clog the hair follicle, while blackheads result from the presence of oxidized melanin in the blocked pores.

1.2.2 Papules and Pustules:

Papules and pustules, commonly referred to as pimples, are small red or white bumps that can be tender to touch. Papules refer to inflamed lesions with no visible pus, whereas pustules are characterized by the presence of pus.

1.2.3 Nodules and Cysts:

Nodular and cystic acne are more severe forms of acne. Nodules are hard, painful, and deep-seated lesions, while cysts are larger and pus-filled. These types often leave behind stubborn scars and require more intensive treatment.

Chapter 2: Preventive Measures for Acne and Blemishes

Proactively adopting a skincare routine built around preventing acne and blemishes is crucial. In this chapter, we will explore a range of preventive measures, highlighting the importance of maintaining a healthy lifestyle and implementing effective skincare practices.

2.1 Cleanse and Exfoliate:

Regularly cleansing your face with a gentle cleanser helps remove excess oil, dirt, and dead skin cells that can clog pores. Exfoliation aids in removing dead skin cells and unclogging the pores, promoting healthy skin cell turnover. However, it is essential to strike a balance, as excessive cleansing and exfoliation can irritate the skin and worsen acne.

2.2 Moisturize:

Many mistakenly believe that moisturizers should be avoided when battling acne. This couldn't be further from the truth. While oily and acne-prone skin should opt for lightweight, non-comedogenic moisturizers, it is vital to keep the skin hydrated. Proper hydration helps maintain the skin's barrier function, preventing excessive oil production.

2.3 Healthy Diet and Lifestyle:

A balanced diet rich in essential nutrients, including fruits, vegetables, whole grains, and lean proteins, can contribute to healthier skin. Foods high in refined carbohydrates and unhealthy fats may exacerbate acne. Regular exercise, sufficient sleep, and stress management techniques are also crucial for skin health, as they help regulate hormonal balance and reduce stress-induced inflammation.

2.4 Sun Protection:

Sun exposure can worsen acne and lead to hyperpigmentation, making sun protection vital. Utilize a broad-spectrum sunscreen with an SPF of at least 30 and apply it generously before stepping outside. Additionally, consider wearing a wide-brimmed hat and seeking shade whenever possible.

Chapter 3: Over-the-Counter (OTC) Treatments for Acne and Blemishes

Over-the-counter products serve as a convenient starting point for treating acne and blemishes. In this chapter, we will explore various OTC treatments and highlight their effectiveness in combating mild to moderate acne.

3.1 Topical Acne Medications:

OTC acne treatments usually contain active ingredients such as benzoyl peroxide or salicylic acid. Benzoyl peroxide aids in reducing acne-causing bacteria, unblocking pores, and minimizing inflammation. Salicylic acid helps exfoliate the skin, unclog pores, and prevent further breakouts. It is crucial to follow the directions carefully to avoid excessive irritation or drying of the skin.

3.2 Retinoids:

Retinoids, derived from vitamin A, are potent agents that enhance skin cell turnover and reduce oil production. OTC retinoids such as adapalene, tazarotene, and retinol are available to help combat acne. These products work best when used consistently over a prolonged period but may cause skin irritation for some, necessitating cautious use.

3.3 Natural Remedies:

While scientific evidence supporting the efficacy of natural remedies for acne may be limited, certain ingredients have demonstrated potential benefits. Tea tree oil possesses antibacterial properties, while aloe vera soothes inflammation and promotes healing. However, it is important to conduct a patch test before using natural remedies and to consult a dermatologist if adverse reactions occur.

Chapter 4: Professional Interventions for Acne and Blemishes

Sometimes, acne and blemishes persist despite diligent skincare and OTC treatments. Seeking professional intervention is essential to address severe acne and prevent long-term skin damage. In this chapter, we will explore such professional treatment options.

4.1 Prescription Medications:

For moderate to severe acne that does not respond to OTC treatments, dermatologists may prescribe oral or topical medications. These can include antibiotics, hormonal treatments for women, or stronger topical retinoids. It is crucial to follow the dermatologist's instructions and attend regular check-ups to monitor any potential side effects.

4.2 Chemical Peels:

Chemical peels involve the application of a chemical solution to the skin, initiating controlled exfoliation and promoting new skin regeneration. They can be effective in improving acne scars and reducing active acne lesions. Chemical peels should be performed by a qualified professional to avoid complications.

4.3 Microdermabrasion and Dermabrasion:

Microdermabrasion and dermabrasion procedures involve mechanically exfoliating the skin using microcrystals or a rotating brush. These treatments aid in removing dead skin cells and reducing the appearance of acne scars. However, they may not be suitable for all skin types, and multiple sessions may be required to achieve optimal results.

Chapter 5: Addressing Blemishes: Coverage and Prevention

While treating acne is essential, addressing blemishes and postinflammatory hyperpigmentation (PIH) is equally crucial. In this chapter, we will explore techniques for concealing blemishes and discuss ways to prevent PIH.

5.1 Makeup and Concealing:

Various makeup products, such as color-correcting primers, concealer, and foundation, can effectively camouflage blemishes. Opt for non-comedogenic, oil-free formulations to avoid clogging pores. Makeup should be removed thoroughly at the end of the day to prevent buildup and further skin irritation.

5.2 Prevention of PIH:

To prevent PIH, avoid picking or squeezing acne lesions, as this can exacerbate inflammation and increase the likelihood of scarring. Adhering to a consistent skincare routine, using SPF daily, and avoiding excessive sun exposure are vital in preventing post-acne dark spots and hyperpigmentation.

By gaining a comprehensive understanding of acne and blemishes, implementing preventative measures, utilizing OTC treatments appropriately, seeking professional intervention when necessary, and addressing blemishes correctly, you can unlock the path to clearer, healthier skin. With dedication and patience, achieving the radiant complexion you desire is within reach.

Exploring Herbal Cosmetics and Skincare

In recent years, herbal cosmetics and skincare have gained tremendous popularity as people are increasingly seeking natural and organic options for their beauty routines. The use of plant-based ingredients has been prevalent for thousands of years in traditional medicine and beauty practices. In this chapter, we embark on an exciting journey to explore the fascinating world of herbal cosmetics and skincare.

A Historical Perspective:

The use of herbal ingredients in cosmetics traces back to ancient civilizations, where various plant extracts and herbs were used to beautify and enhance the skin. Cleopatra, the iconic Egyptian queen, was renowned for her skincare regimen, which included luxurious herbal baths and facial treatments. Egyptians effectively utilized natural ingredients like aloe vera, rosemary, and chamomile for their soothing effects on the skin and hair.

In traditional Chinese medicine, a holistic approach is followed, emphasizing the balance of energy, or qi, in the body. Herbal ingredients like ginseng, green tea, and licorice root have long been incorporated into skincare to promote healthy complexion and combat signs of aging.

India also has a rich history of herbal cosmetics and skincare with Ayurveda—a system of medicine that emphasizes a balance between body, mind, and spirit. Ayurvedic beauty rituals often include the use of ingredients such as sandalwood, neem, turmeric, and amla to cleanse, moisturize, and rejuvenate the skin.

The Science Behind Herbal Cosmetics:

Herbal cosmetics derive their efficacy from the bioactive compounds present in plants. These compounds possess multiple beneficial properties such as antioxidant, anti-inflammatory, antimicrobial, and moisturizing effects. Engaging with nature's pharmacy, herbal cosmetics harness these properties to offer a range of benefits for the skin and hair.

For instance, aloe vera, a popular herbal ingredient, contains polysaccharides that promote hydration and soothe irritated skin. The gel extracted from aloe vera leaves is often used in moisturizers, cleansers, and sunscreens due to its ability to reduce inflammation and support healing.

Green tea, another widely used herbal ingredient, is packed with polyphenols and catechins that exhibit potent antioxidant properties. These components help protect the skin from oxidative stress, reduce signs of aging, and improve overall skin health.

Herbal Ingredients for Skincare:

The plethora of herbal ingredients available for skincare can be overwhelming, so let's delve into the most notable ones:

1. Lavender: Known for its calming effects, lavender oil is commonly used in skincare products to reduce redness and inflammation. It also has antimicrobial properties, making it an excellent choice for acne-prone skin.

2. Chamomile: Extracts from chamomile flowers are often used in cosmetics due to their soothing and anti-inflammatory effects. This herbal ingredient is gentle on the skin, making it suitable for sensitive skin types.

3. Rosehip: Rich in vitamins A and C, rosehip oil helps improve the texture, tone, and elasticity of the skin. It is also known to reduce the appearance of scars and rejuvenate dull-looking skin.

4. Calendula: Calendula extract is often incorporated into skincare products for its wound-healing properties. It has a soothing effect on the skin and helps reduce redness and irritation.

5. Turmeric: This vibrant yellow spice is well-known for its anti-inflammatory and antioxidant properties. Turmeric helps combat free radicals, brightens the skin, and reduces blemishes.

Herbal Ingredients for Haircare:

In addition to skincare, herbal ingredients offer numerous benefits for hair health. Let's explore a few key ingredients:

1. Amla: Also known as Indian gooseberry, amla is rich in vitamin C and antioxidants. It nourishes the scalp, promotes hair growth, and strengthens hair follicles, reducing hair fall.

2. Hibiscus: Hibiscus extract is often used in herbal hair care products to control dandruff, prevent hair loss, and promote shiny, healthy locks. It also helps condition and moisturize the scalp.

3. Peppermint: Known for its refreshing scent, peppermint oil increases blood circulation to the scalp, promoting hair growth and reducing scalp irritation.

4. Rosemary: Rosemary oil can stimulate hair follicles, strengthen hair strands, and delay premature graying. Its antibacterial properties can also help combat dandruff.
Exploring the world of herbal cosmetics and skincare allows us to discover the incredible benefits that nature has to offer for our beauty needs. From ancient civilizations to modern science, the use of plant-based ingredients continues to occupy a prominent place in our quest for healthier, more sustainable beauty products. As we continue this journey, we'll uncover a treasure trove of herbal ingredients and their countless benefits for our skin and hair.

Chapter 10: Herbal Remedies for Respiratory Ailments

In this chapter, we will explore the fascinating world of herbal remedies for respiratory ailments. Our respiratory system plays a vital rolc in bringing oxygen into our bodies and expelling harmful carbon dioxide. However, this complex system is susceptible to various ailments, including common colds, bronchitis, asthma, and allergies. While medical treatments are widely available, many individuals seek natural alternatives to help alleviate their respiratory troubles. Herbal remedies, derived from plants with therapeutic properties, have been used for centuries to address respiratory ailments. Let us delve into the rich tradition of herbal medicine and discover some potent herbs that can provide relief and promote respiratory health.

1. Eucalyptus (Eucalyptus globulus):

Eucalyptus, native to Australia, is renowned for its refreshing fragrance and numerous health benefits. Its leaves are distilled to extract the essential oil, which is commonly used in respiratory treatments. The oil contains a compound called eucalyptol, which possesses expectorant and decongestant properties. Inhalation of eucalyptus oil can help clear nasal passages, relieve coughs, and reduce inflammation. You can benefit from eucalyptus by using it as a steam inhalation, adding a few drops to a diffuser, or applying a diluted oil topically on the chest.

2. Peppermint (Mentha piperita):

Peppermint, known for its cooling sensation and distinct aroma, offers an array of health benefits, including respiratory support. The menthol present in peppermint leaves acts as a relaxant, particularly for the muscles in the respiratory system. This relaxation can help reduce coughing and open up airways, making it easier to breathe. Peppermint tea is a popular herbal remedy for congestion and respiratory discomfort. Additionally, inhaling peppermint oil or using a topical balm can help soothe nasal passages and relieve sinus headaches.

3. Licorice Root (Glycyrrhiza glabra):

Licorice root has been used in traditional medicine for its anti-inflammatory and expectorant properties. It contains glycyrrhizin, a compound believed to reduce airway inflammation and soothe irritation in the lungs. Licorice root tea is a common remedy for coughs, bronchitis, and throat irritations. However, it's important to note that excessive consumption of licorice root or prolonged use can lead to side effects, hence moderation is advised. Consult a healthcare professional before incorporating licorice root into your respiratory regimen.

4. Mullein (Verbascum thapsus):

Mullein, also known as "nature's respiratory remedy," has long been used to soothe various respiratory ailments. The leaves and flowers of this plant are used to prepare herbal remedies that can alleviate congestion, dry coughs, and bronchial spasms. Mullein tea is a popular choice for individuals seeking relief from asthma, bronchitis, and sore throats. Its anti-inflammatory properties are believed to help reduce inflammation in the respiratory tract, making breathing more comfortable.

5. Thyme (Thymus vulgaris):

Thyme is not only a popular culinary herb but also a powerful medicinal plant with respiratory benefits. Thyme leaves contain compounds, such as thymol, that possess antiseptic and expectorant properties. These properties make thyme an excellent herb for treating respiratory infections, coughs, and congestion. Drinking thyme tea or inhaling its steam can help decongest nasal passages and soothe irritated airways. Thyme honey is also highly regarded for its ability to relieve coughs and sore throats.

6. Marshmallow Root (Althaea officinalis):

Marshmallow root has a long history of use in traditional medicine, especially for respiratory ailments. Its mucilaginous properties provide a soothing effect on irritated tissues. The root is commonly brewed into a tea, which can help relieve coughs, bronchitis, and irritated throat conditions. Marshmallow root may also help reduce inflammation in the respiratory tract, encouraging easier breathing.

7. Osha Root (Ligusticum porteri):

Osha root, native to the Rocky Mountains, has been used for centuries by Native American tribes to aid respiratory health. It is celebrated for its ability to relieve coughs, sinus congestion, and bronchial infections. Osha root contains camphor and other compounds that possess expectorant and anti-inflammatory properties. The root is commonly consumed as a tincture or brewed into a tea to promote respiratory wellness.

8. Ginger (Zingiber officinale):

Ginger, well-known for its medicinal properties, offers respiratory benefits as well. Its warming and anti-inflammatory properties make it a valuable herb for soothing respiratory discomfort. Ginger can help alleviate coughs, relieve congestion, and support immune function. Ginger tea, made from fresh ginger root, is a popular remedy for colds, flu, and sore throats. The addition of honey and lemon can enhance its soothing effects.

Exploring the realm of herbal remedies for respiratory ailments reveals the vast array of beneficial plants available to support respiratory health. Eucalyptus, peppermint, licorice root, mullein, thyme, marshmallow root, osha root, and ginger are just a few examples of potent herbs that can provide relief and promote well-being.

While herbal remedies can offer natural alternatives, it is important to remember that they should not replace professional medical advice. It is recommended to consult a healthcare professional before incorporating herbal treatments into your respiratory regimen, especially if you have pre-existing medical conditions or are taking medications.

By combining the knowledge of traditional medicine with modern scientific research, we can explore the world of herbal remedies and harness their potential to support our respiratory system's health.

Easing Congestion and Respiratory Infections

In today's fast-paced world, respiratory infections and congestion have become prevalent issues affecting a large portion of the population. As individuals strive to meet their daily responsibilities, they often neglect their well-being, inadvertently compromising their immune system's ability to fight against infections. Additionally, factors such as air pollution, stress, and the presence of airborne pathogens in crowded areas contribute to the rise in respiratory infections. Therefore, it is crucial to explore effective strategies to ease congestion and minimize the risk of contracting respiratory infections. In this chapter, we will delve into various preventive measures, natural remedies, and lifestyle modification techniques to address these concerns.

Understanding Respiratory Infections:

Respiratory infections are illnesses that primarily affect the respiratory tract, including the throat, lungs, and nasal passages. Common examples include the common cold, influenza, bronchitis, and pneumonia. These infections can be caused by viruses or bacteria, and their transmission often occurs through airborne droplets expelled from infected individuals when they cough or sneeze. In crowded places or enclosed environments, such as public transport, workplaces, or schools, the risk of contracting respiratory infections increases significantly.

Preventing Respiratory Infections:

Prevention is always better than cure when it comes to respiratory infections. While it is impossible to completely eliminate the risk, adopting certain preventive measures can help reduce the likelihood of infection. The most effective way to prevent respiratory infections is by practicing good hygiene techniques. These include:

1. Frequent handwashing: Regularly washing hands with soap and water for at least 20 seconds can eliminate many disease-causing germs and viruses.
2. Using hand sanitizers: When soap and water are not readily available, alcohol-based hand sanitizers can be an effective alternative.
3. Covering mouth and nose: Using tissues or the crook of an elbow when coughing or sneezing can reduce the transmission of pathogens from person to person.
4. Avoiding close contact with sick individuals: Maintaining a safe distance from someone exhibiting respiratory symptoms is crucial, as direct contact increases the risk of infection.

Moreover, maintaining a robust immune system can play a significant role in preventing respiratory infections. A healthy lifestyle that incorporates regular exercise, a balanced diet, and plenty of restorative sleep can strengthen the immune system, making it more equipped to combat infections.

Natural Remedies for Respiratory Congestion:

Congestion is a common symptom accompanying respiratory infections. It causes discomfort and can hinder daily activities. While over-the-counter medications are available to alleviate congestion temporarily, natural remedies can often provide relief without any side effects. Here are some effective natural remedies for easing congestion:

1. Steam inhalation: Inhaling steam from a bowl of hot water or taking a hot shower can help loosen mucus and clear congested airways.
2. Eucalyptus oil: Adding a few drops of eucalyptus oil to hot water and inhaling the steam can provide soothing relief and aid decongestion.
3. Nasal irrigation: Using a neti pot or saline nasal spray can help rinse out excess mucus and reduce nasal congestion.
4. Warm compress: Applying a warm compress over the sinus area can effectively alleviate congestion and sinus pressure.

Lifestyle Modification:
In addition to preventive measures and natural remedies, certain lifestyle modifications can enhance overall respiratory health and minimize the risk of infections. Consider the following:

1. Improving indoor air quality: Many respiratory infections are caused or exacerbated by poor indoor air quality. Regularly cleaning and vacuuming the house, using air purifiers, and ensuring proper ventilation can significantly reduce the concentration of airborne

pollutants and allergens.

2. Avoiding smoke exposure: Cigarette smoke, both active and passive, significantly increases the risk of respiratory infections. Quitting smoking and avoiding exposure to secondhand smoke can have a positive impact on overall respiratory health.

3. Strengthening immune system through nutrition: Adopting a diet rich in vitamins, minerals, and antioxidants helps boost the immune system. Incorporating fruits, vegetables, whole grains, and lean proteins into daily meals can provide the necessary nutrients to fight against infections.

4. Managing stress: Chronic stress weakens the immune system and increases susceptibility to respiratory infections. Engaging in stress-reducing activities such as yoga, meditation, or hobbies can help alleviate stress and promote overall well-being.

Respiratory infections and congestion can have a significant impact on an individual's quality of life and productivity. However, by adopting preventive measures, utilizing natural remedies, and implementing lifestyle modifications, it is possible to alleviate congestion and minimize the risk of contracting respiratory infections. These strategies not only provide immediate relief but also promote long-term respiratory health, allowing individuals to thrive in their personal and professional lives. Remember, taking care of one's respiratory system is just as important as any other aspect of maintaining overall well-being.

Herbs for Soothing Coughs and Sore Throats

Coughs and sore throats are common ailments that can leave us feeling miserable and uncomfortable. Whether caused by a cold, allergies, or other respiratory infections, these conditions disrupt our daily lives and affect our overall well-being. While over-the-counter medications can provide relief, many people are turning to herbal remedies as a natural and effective alternative. In this chapter, we will explore a variety of herbs that have been traditionally used for soothing coughs and sore throats, providing you with safe and effective options for alleviating these bothersome symptoms.

1. Peppermint (Mentha piperita):

Peppermint is a versatile herb that is cherished for its refreshing aroma and cooling properties. When it comes to soothing coughs and sore throats, peppermint's menthol content acts as a natural decongestant, breaking up mucus and relieving respiratory congestion. Its antispasmodic properties also help calm dry and irritating coughs, providing both comfort and relief. To harness the benefits of peppermint, you can steep its leaves in hot water to make a soothing tea or gargle with a diluted peppermint essential oil mixture to alleviate a sore throat.

2. Echinacea (Echinacea purpurea):

Echinacea, also known as the purple coneflower, has long been used by Native Americans for its immune-boosting properties. It contains compounds that help strengthen the body's defenses, making it an excellent herb for fighting off respiratory infections that often accompany coughs and sore throats. Echinacea is available in various forms, such as capsules, tinctures, and teas, allowing you to choose the most convenient option to suit your needs.

3. Marshmallow Root (Althaea officinalis):

Marshmallow root is a demulcent herb known for its soothing and protective properties. It forms a gel-like substance when mixed with water, which coats the throat, alleviates inflammation, and reduces irritation caused by coughing. Drinking marshmallow root tea or using it as a gargle can provide relief for both coughs and sore throats. It is worth noting that marshmallow root may interact with certain medications, so consulting with a healthcare professional is advisable before incorporating it into your routine.

4. Licorice Root (Glycyrrhiza glabra):

Licorice root, with its distinct sweet flavor, has been utilized for centuries in traditional medicine. It boasts potent anti-inflammatory and expectorant properties, making it an ideal herb for relieving both dry and productive coughs. Licorice root helps soothe the respiratory tract, ease throat irritation, and promote mucus production, aiding in the expulsion of phlegm. As licorice root can elevate blood pressure when consumed in large amounts, it is important to consume it in moderation and consult with a healthcare professional if you have pre-existing conditions.

5. Slippery Elm (Ulmus rubra):

The inner bark of the slippery elm tree has been used for centuries to soothe various ailments, including coughs and sore throats. Its high mucilage content forms a protective layer in the throat, reducing irritation and alleviating both dry and hoarse coughs. Slippery elm can be consumed as a tea or mixed with honey to create a soothing syrup for sore throats. It is essential to note that slippery elm may interfere with the absorption of medications, so it is advisable to take it separately from any prescribed medications.

6. Thyme (Thymus vulgaris):

Thyme is a versatile herb widely used in culinary dishes, but it also possesses remarkable medicinal properties. Its active compounds, like thymol, exhibit expectorant and antimicrobial effects, making it a valuable herb for soothing coughs and combatting respiratory infections. Thyme tea can be prepared by steeping the leaves in hot water, providing relief for coughs and helping to clear congestion. Its aromatic scent also works as a natural decongestant, facilitating easier breathing during episodes of respiratory distress.

7. Sage (Salvia officinalis):

Sage, a herb known for its culinary uses, also offers medicinal benefits for respiratory health. Its antimicrobial and anti-inflammatory properties make it a valuable ally against respiratory infections that can lead to coughs and sore throats. Sage tea or gargling with a sage infusion can significantly reduce throat pain and inflammation while helping to soothe persistent coughs.

8. Mullein (Verbascum thapsus):

Mullein is a herbaceous plant widely known for its soft leaves and tall flowers. It possesses expectorant properties, making it an excellent herb for expelling mucus and alleviating coughs. Mullein tea, prepared by steeping the dried leaves in hot water, can help reduce coughing fits and soothe irritated throats. Additionally, mullein leaves can be used to create a poultice for topical application on the chest to relieve congestion.

9. Ginger (Zingiber officinale):

Ginger is a well-known herb revered for its digestive and anti-inflammatory properties. When it comes to coughs and sore throats, ginger's warming and soothing effects make it a valuable addition to any herbal remedy. Drinking ginger tea or adding ginger to warm water with honey is an effective way to alleviate throat discomfort and reduce coughing. Ginger's antimicrobial properties may also help combat underlying infections that contribute to these symptoms.

Asthma and Allergy Management through Herbs

In recent years, the prevalence of asthma and allergies has significantly increased, affecting millions of individuals worldwide. This rise in respiratory conditions is often attributed to various environmental factors, such as pollution, chemicals, and allergens. While modern medicine has made significant advancements in treating these conditions, many individuals seek alternative approaches to manage their symptoms and reduce their reliance on pharmaceutical drugs. The use of herbs in asthma and allergy management has garnered considerable attention due to their potential therapeutic properties. In this chapter, we will explore the role of herbs in managing asthma and allergies, highlighting their benefits, recommended usage, and potential side effects.

Understanding Asthma and Allergies:

Asthma, a chronic respiratory condition, is characterized by inflamed bronchial tubes and reduced airflow, leading to symptoms such as wheezing, coughing, and shortness of breath. Allergies, on the other hand, occur when the immune system reacts to certain substances, known as allergens, triggering symptoms like sneezing, itching, and congestion. It is important to note that while asthma and allergies are distinct conditions, they often coexist, and managing them requires a comprehensive approach.

Benefits of Herbs in Asthma and Allergy Management:

1. Anti-inflammatory Effects: Many herbs possess potent anti-inflammatory properties, which can help alleviate the bronchial inflammation associated with asthma. Examples of anti-inflammatory herbs include turmeric, ginger, boswellia, and licorice root. These herbs can potentially reduce the severity and frequency of asthma attacks.

2. Antihistamine Properties: Allergies are predominantly caused by an immune response triggered by histamine release. Certain herbs, such as stinging nettle, butterbur, and elderflower, possess natural antihistamine properties, inhibiting the release of histamine and reducing allergic symptoms like sneezing and itching.

3. Immune Modulation: Some herbs, including astragalus, echinacea, and garlic, are known for their immune-modulating properties. These herbs may enhance the immune system's response to allergens, reducing the severity of allergic reactions.

4. Bronchodilation: Herbs like eucalyptus, peppermint, and thyme have been traditionally used to support bronchodilation, helping to open up airways and ease breathing difficulties associated with asthma.

Herbal Recommendations for Asthma and Allergy Management:

1. Boswellia (Boswellia serrata): Boswellia, also known as Indian frankincense, has been used for centuries in Ayurvedic medicine for its anti-inflammatory properties. It may help reduce bronchial inflammation and improve respiratory function, making it potentially beneficial for asthma management.

2. Turmeric (Curcuma longa): Curcumin, the active compound in turmeric, possesses strong anti-inflammatory properties. It can potentially alleviate airway inflammation and reduce asthma symptoms. Combining turmeric with black pepper can enhance its absorption and efficacy.

3. Stinging Nettle (Urtica dioica): Stinging nettle has natural antihistamine properties, making it effective in managing allergic symptoms. It can be consumed in the form of tea or as a supplement, but precautions should be taken to avoid contact with fresh nettle leaves, which can cause skin irritation.

4. Butterbur (Petasites hybridus): Butterbur is another herb commonly used for its antihistamine effects. It may help reduce allergic symptoms such as nasal congestion and sneezing. However, it is essential to use only certified toxin-free butterbur products, as this plant contains potentially harmful alkaloids.

5. Licorice Root (Glycyrrhiza glabra): With its anti-inflammatory properties, licorice root may help reduce bronchial inflammation and soothe irritated airways in asthma. However, due to its potential side effects, long-term use should be avoided or approached cautiously under professional guidance.

Potential Side Effects and Precautions:

While herbs can offer potential relief for asthma and allergies, it is crucial to exercise caution, especially when using them as complementary therapy alongside conventional treatments. Some herbs may interact with medications or cause adverse effects. For instance, licorice root can increase blood pressure and lead to electrolyte imbalances if used in excess. Therefore, it is advisable to consult a qualified healthcare practitioner before integrating herbs into your asthma and allergy management plan.

Additionally, some herbs may not be suitable for certain individuals, such as pregnant or lactating women, children, and individuals with underlying medical conditions. Allergies to specific herbs should also be considered, as they can cause severe reactions in susceptible individuals.

The utilization of herbs in asthma and allergy management provides an alternative approach for individuals seeking additional relief from their symptoms. It is vital to remember that herbs should not be seen as standalone treatments but rather as complementary options to conventional medical management. By understanding the benefits, recommended usage, and potential side effects of various herbs, individuals can make informed decisions regarding their asthma and allergy management. As always, professional guidance and collaboration between herbalists and healthcare practitioners are crucial to ensure the utmost safety and efficacy in integrating herbs into existing treatment regimens.

Traditional vs. Modern Approaches to Lung Health

In recent times, the importance of maintaining a healthy respiratory system has become increasingly evident. Our lungs are responsible for inhaling vital oxygen and expelling harmful carbon dioxide, ensuring the proper functioning of our body. However, with the rise of pollution levels, sedentary lifestyles, and unhealthy habits, respiratory issues have also climbed the ranks as one of the leading causes of mortality and morbidity worldwide. In the quest for superior lung health, two distinctive approaches have emerged – the traditional and the modern. In this chapter, we will explore the differing beliefs, therapeutic techniques, and methodologies utilized by each approach and consider the benefits and drawbacks they possess.

Traditional Approaches to Lung Health:

1. Ayurveda and Traditional Chinese Medicine:

Ancient civilizations across the globe recognized the importance of healthy lungs and developed methods to maintain their optimal functioning. Ayurveda, a holistic system of medicine originating in India, emphasizes the balance of bodily elements. According to Ayurvedic principles, maintaining a state of harmony between the three doshas: Vata, Pitta, and Kapha, is vital for lung health. The system recommends a holistic approach, including dietary changes, herbal remedies, and yogic practices, to promote healing and enhance lung function.

Traditional Chinese Medicine (TCM), which dates back thousands of years, believes that lung health is closely intertwined with the flow of Qi, the vital energy within our bodies. TCM utilizes acupuncture, herbal medicine, and specific breathing exercises to improve lung function and treat ailments such as respiratory infections, asthma, and chronic obstructive pulmonary disease (COPD). The practice also stresses the importance of balancing yin and yang energies for optimal lung health.

2. Indigenous Healing Methods:

Indigenous cultures worldwide have long relied on their traditional healing practices to maintain lung health. Native American tribes, for instance, employ smudging rituals using herbs like sage, cedar, and sweetgrass to purify the air and promote respiratory wellness. In Australian Aboriginal culture, traditional medicine is based on the usage of native plants, such as eucalyptus and tea tree, known for their antibacterial and expectorant properties.

These traditional approaches, deeply rooted in cultural wisdom and passed down through generations, embody a holistic view of health, acknowledging the connection between the physical body, the mind, and the environment. However, while these methods have shown promise, they are often dismissed by modern medical practitioners due to a lack of scientific evidence and standardized studies.

Modern Approaches to Lung Health:

1. Conventional Medicine:

Conventional medicine, heavily built upon scientific research and evidence-based practice, relies on pharmaceutical interventions and surgical procedures to treat respiratory ailments. In cases of infection, antibiotics are prescribed to eliminate bacteria causing respiratory distress. For chronic conditions like asthma or COPD, bronchodilators and corticosteroids often form the cornerstone of treatment. In severe cases, lung transplantation may be necessary to improve lung function and enhance overall quality of life.

Conventional medicine's emphasis on advanced diagnostic tools, such as X-rays, CT scans, and spirometry, provides medical professionals with precise information to identify and manage lung diseases effectively. While modern medicine offers faster relief and interventions, some argue that it often neglects the holistic approach favored by traditional methods.

2. Technological Advancements:

With the rapid advancement of technology, medical innovations have revolutionized the diagnosis and treatment of respiratory conditions. Pulmonary function tests, pulse oximeters, and pulmonary rehabilitation programs are just a few examples of modern approaches to promoting lung health. Innovative devices like inhalers, nebulizers, and oxygen therapy equipment have also significantly improved the management of chronic respiratory diseases, allowing patients to lead more fulfilling lives.

Moreover, telemedicine has emerged as a convenient method for consultation and monitoring of lung health. Remote monitoring of respiratory parameters and virtual healthcare platforms have facilitated access to specialist care, particularly in rural and underserved areas. The integration of artificial intelligence and machine learning algorithms in the medical field holds the potential for more precise diagnoses and personalized treatment plans tailored to individual patients.

The battle between traditional and modern approaches to lung health continues, each offering distinct benefits and challenges. Traditional methods emphasize the importance of holistic wellness, focusing on the mind-body connection and utilizing natural remedies. Conversely, modern approaches rely on scientific advancements, offering precision diagnostics and interventions that provide faster relief. While both approaches have their merits, a balanced integration of both could potentially optimize respiratory health even further.

Herbs for Heart and Circulatory Health

In this chapter, we delve into the fascinating world of herbs that promote heart and circulatory health. The heart is undoubtedly one of the most vital organs in the human body, responsible for pumping oxygen-rich blood to all the cells and organs. It is no wonder that maintaining a healthy heart is of paramount importance for overall well-being. While conventional medicine offers various treatments for heart-related issues, traditional herbal remedies have been used for centuries to support heart health. This chapter explores some of the most well-known and effective herbs used for maintaining a strong and vibrant heart.

1. Hawthorn (Crataegus spp.):

Hawthorn has long been revered for its benefits to heart health and is amongst the most widely studied herbs in this field. It has a rich history of use dating back to ancient Greece and has been recognized for its ability to support healthy blood pressure levels and improve circulation. Hawthorn contains potent antioxidants that reduce oxidative stress on the heart, protecting it from damage caused by free radicals. Studies have shown that hawthorn can help enhance the strength of heart contractions, regulate heart rhythm, and improve overall cardiovascular health.

2. Garlic (Allium sativum):

Present in kitchens worldwide, garlic is not only a tasty ingredient but also an essential herb for heart health. Garlic contains a compound called allicin, which has been shown to lower blood pressure, reduce cholesterol levels, and prevent blood clot formation. Additionally, garlic has anti-inflammatory properties that alleviate inflammation in the arteries, reduce plaque buildup, and promote healthy circulation. Regular consumption of garlic has been associated with a decreased risk of heart disease and stroke.

3. Ginger (Zingiber officinale):

A favorite spice in many cuisines, ginger has been used for centuries to support cardiovascular health. Compounds such as gingerol, shogaol, and zingerone in ginger have potent anti-inflammatory and antioxidant properties, which help in maintaining heart health. Ginger aids in lowering cholesterol levels, preventing blood clot formation, and reducing blood pressure levels. By improving blood flow and reducing inflammation within the arteries, ginger can significantly reduce the risk of developing heart-related conditions.

4. Turmeric (Curcuma longa):

This bright yellow spice, commonly found in curries, contains curcumin, a compound responsible for turmeric's impressive health benefits. Curcumin has potent anti-inflammatory properties that can help reduce inflammation in the blood vessels, lower cholesterol, and prevent blood clot formation. Turmeric also protects the heart by improving endothelial function, increasing nitric oxide production, and decreasing oxidative stress. Including turmeric in one's diet or opting for curcumin supplements can contribute to maintaining a healthy heart.

5. Ginkgo (Ginkgo biloba):

Though primarily known for its cognitive benefits, ginkgo also offers advantages for heart health. This ancient herb improves circulation by dilating blood vessels and thinning the blood, reducing the likelihood of clots. Ginkgo contains flavonoids and terpenoids, which act as antioxidants, protecting the heart from damage caused by oxidative stress. Moreover, it enhances the delivery of oxygen and nutrients to the heart, boosting overall cardiovascular health.

6. Danshen (Salvia miltiorrhiza):

Danshen, also known as red sage, is a traditional Chinese herb that has been used to support heart health for thousands of years. It contains active compounds called tanshinones, which possess antioxidant, anti-inflammatory, and vasodilatory properties. Danshen helps to improve blood flow, reduce blood pressure, and prevent platelet aggregation. It has also been shown to improve coronary artery circulation and protect against heart damage caused by ischemia.

7. Motherwort (Leonurus cardiaca):

True to its name, motherwort has long been used to strengthen and support women's heart health. It is an excellent herb for maintaining cardiovascular health in both men and women. Motherwort contains alkaloids that help regulate heartbeat rhythm, preventing arrhythmias and palpitations. Additionally, it helps to calm the nervous system and reduce anxiety, indirectly supporting heart health. This herb is known for its ability to strengthen the heart muscle, improving its pumping efficiency.

8. Yarrow (Achillea millefolium):

Yarrow is an herb widely known for its ability to promote healthy blood circulation. It has a long history of use in traditional medicine for issues related to the heart and circulatory system. Yarrow contains flavonoids, tannins, and volatile oils that help dilate blood vessels, reduce inflammation, and prevent blood clot formation. It is also known to reduce blood pressure and strengthen the walls of fragile blood vessels. These properties make yarrow an excellent herb for maintaining optimal cardiovascular health.

9. Cayenne (Capsicum annuum):

Cayenne, a fiery spice, possesses a host of cardiovascular benefits. It contains a compound called capsaicin that enhances blood circulation by expanding blood vessels and improving blood flow. Cayenne also helps reduce blood pressure levels and prevent the formation of blood clots. Additionally, it aids in strengthening the heart muscle and balancing cholesterol levels, contributing to a healthier heart.

10. Olive Leaf (Olea europaea):

Perhaps best known for its association with olive oil, the leaves of the olive tree also hold tremendous heart-protective properties. Olive leaf extract contains a compound called oleuropein, which has potent antioxidant and anti-inflammatory effects. It reduces blood pressure, improves endothelial function, and prevents platelet aggregation, minimizing the risk of heart disease. Including olive leaf extract in one's daily routine can significantly promote heart and circulatory health.

In this chapter, we have explored a multitude of herbs that play a crucial role in maintaining heart and circulatory health. The natural remedies discussed, including hawthorn, garlic, ginger, turmeric, ginkgo, danshen, motherwort, yarrow, cayenne, and olive leaf, offer incredible benefits backed by both traditional knowledge and scientific research. Although these herbs can complement conventional treatment, it is essential to consult with a healthcare professional before incorporating them into your daily routine, especially if you have pre-existing heart conditions or are taking medications. With the guidance of a healthcare expert, herbs can be powerful allies in our quest for a strong and vibrant heart.